As "cover girl," officer manager of Bon Vivant Press

and owner of authors Robert and Kathleen Fish,

I would like to share the joys of our vacations and working

trips to produce our *Cooking Secrets* series.

Special thanks to my bon vivant canine pals,

Page, Rocky and Joey.

– Dreamer Dawg

PACIFIC NORTHWEST

Pets Welcome

A Guide to Hotels, Inns and Resorts That Welcome You and Your Pet

KATHLEEN AND ROBERT FISH

BON VIVANT

Library of Congress Cataloging-in-Publication Data
Pets Welcome™ Pacific Northwest
A Guide to Hotels, Inns and Resorts
That Welcome You and Your Pet

Fish, Kathleen DeVanna
Fish, Robert N.
97-077737
ISBN 1-883214-25-4
$15.95 softcover
Includes indexes

9/12/12   *15.95*

Cover photography by Robert N. Fish
Editorial direction by Judie Marks
Editorial assistance by Nadine Guarrera and Susan Parkes
Cover design by Abalone Design Group
Illustrations by Krishna Gopa, Graphic Design & Illustration and
Gerrica Connolly, Design Studio
Type by Masterproof

Published by Bon Vivant Press
a division of The Millennium Publishing Group
P.O. Box 1994
Monterey, CA 93942

Printed in the United States of America
by Banta Book Group

Contents

Introduction **6**
Top Ten Travel Tips **7**
Humane Society of the United States:
Traveling With Your Pet **10**
Things You Should Know Before Traveling
To Canada **16**

Map of Oregon **18**
Oregon Inns **19**
Where to Take Your Pet in Oregon **70**

Map of Washington **84**
Washington Inns **85**
Where to Take Your Pet in Washington **148**

Map of British Columbia **160**
British Columbia Inns **161**
Where to Take Your Pet in British
Columbia **200**

Index **215**

❖

Abbreviations Used in this Book

AAA American Automobile Association
ABA American Breeders Association
AKC American Kennel Club
AARP American Association of Retired Persons

Introduction

H ow many vacations have been dampened or cut short over the years because you either couldn't find an appropriate sitter for your beloved pets or you simply couldn't bear to leave them behind? If only you could bring your dog along to explore the wide open spaces of the Pacific Northwest; to wander the cliffs of the Columbia River, hike the wildflower meadows and conifer forests, ford streams when the steelhead run, chase gulls along a sandy beach, retire before a flagstone hearth. . .

You can. And Pets Welcome™ is here to show you how.

We've done the leg-work for you. Thanks to the discovery of myriad three-, four- or five-paw hotels and motels, ranches, spas and bed-and-breakfasts throughout Oregon, Washington and British Columbia, who not only welcome you and your pet, but offer special accommodations, nobody has to stay home.

Pets Welcome™ caters to all kinds of budgets by offering an array of lodging options ranging from the luxurious and romantic to the quirky and rustic. Each location, selected for its ambiance, guest amenities and pet friendliness, has been artfully described, complete with architectural renderings. The summaries provided on each property will enable you to select the ideal location to accommodate the particular travel needs of you and your "best friend." In addition, comprehensive listings of points of interest amenable to both you and your pet are highlighted throughout the guidebook.

Whether you and your pet are seasoned traveling companions or venturing out for the first time, you will be well served by the Humane Society's traveling tips regarding transportation, security and pet care while "on the road." These helpful hints provide insight into traveling by car, plane, boat or train, offering specialized guidance on crating animals, documentation and basic care, Being an informed pet owner will make your trip more enjoyable and comfortable for both you and your pet.

It is our hope and our experience that as you explore the great Pacific Northwest, Pets Welcome™ will become your finest resource and your favorite traveling companion ... well, maybe your second favorite.

Top Ten Travel Tips

1 Bring your pet's own food, dishes, litter and litter box, leash, collar with I.D. tags, a first-aid kit and a bottle of water from home. These will make your pet more comfortable, decrease the chances of an upset stomach from a strange brand of food and help prepare you for emergencies. Maintain the normal feeding and walking schedules as much as possible. Be sure to bring old bath towels or paper towels in case of an accident and plastic bags in which to dispose of your pet's waste. It is a good idea to bring a picture of your pet for identification purposes in case you and your pet become separated.

2 Bring your pet's vaccination records with you when traveling within the state, and a health certificate when traveling out of state. If you plan on boarding him at any time during your vacation, call the kennel to reserve his space, to see what they require you to bring and to find out if they require a health certificate.

3 Bring your pet's favorite toys, leash, grooming supplies, medications, bedding and waste removal supplies. It is a good idea to bring an old sheet or blanket from home to place over the hotel's bedding, just in case your pet gets on the bed. It also will come in handy to protect your car seats from pet hair and dirty paws.

4 Tape the address of where you are staying on the back of your pet's I.D. tag, or add a laminated card or new I.D. tag to your pet's collar, or add a second collar with a friend's or family member's phone number. It is always a good idea to have a second contact person on your pet's collar in case of a natural disaster so that someone out of your area can be contacted if you and your pet become separated.

5 Do not leave your pets unattended in the hotel room. The surroundings are new and unfamiliar to your animal, which may cause him to become upset and destroy property he normally would not, or to bark excessively and disturb your neighbors. You will also run the risk of his escaping. If a maid should open the door to clean your room, the pet may see that as a chance to escape to find you, or he may attack the maid out of fear.

6 Train your pet to accept being in a crate. This will come in handy if you ever need to travel by plane. Make sure the crate has enough room for your pet to stand up comfortably and to turn around inside. Be sure to trim your pet's nails so they don't get caught in the crate door or ventilation holes. Crates come in handy in hotel rooms, too. If your pet is already used to being in a crate, he will not object if you leave him in one long enough to go out to breakfast. Never take your pet with you if you will have to leave him in the car. If it is 85 degrees outside, within minutes the inside of the car can reach over 160 degrees, even with the windows cracked, causing heat stroke and possible death. According to The Humane Society of the United States, the signs of heat stress are: heavy panting, glazed eyes, a rapid pulse, unsteadiness, a staggering gait, vomiting or a deep red or purple tongue. If heat stoke does occur, the pet must be cooled by dousing him with water and applying ice packs to his head and neck. He should then be taken to a veterinarian immediately.

7 When your pet is confined to a crate, the best way to provide water is to freeze it in the cup that hooks onto the door of the crate. That way they will get needed moisture without the water splashing all over the crate. Freezing water in your pet's regular water bowl also works well for car trips.

8 Be sure to put your pet's favorite toys and bedding in the crate. Label the crate with "LIVE ANIMAL" and "THIS END UP," plus the address and phone number of your destination, as well as your home address and phone number and the number of someone to contact in case of an emergency.

9 When traveling by plane be sure to book the most direct flights possible. The less your pet has to be transferred from plane to plane, the less chance of you being separated. This is also very important when traveling in hot or cold weather. You don't want your pet to have to wait in the cargo hold of a plane or be exposed to bad weather any longer than necessary. Check with the airlines for the type of crate they require and any additional requirements. They are very strict about the size and type of crate you may carry on board.

10 Do not feed your pet before traveling. This reduces the risk of an upset stomach or an accident in his crate or your car. When traveling by car, remember that your pet needs rest stops as often as you do. It is a good idea for everyone to stretch their legs from time to time. If your pet is unfamiliar with car travel, then get him accustomed to the car gradually. Start a few weeks before your trip with short trips around town and extend the trips a little each time. Then he will become accustomed to the car before your trip and it will be more pleasant for all involved.

Traveling With Your Pet

Courtesy of The Humane Society of the United States (HSUS)
2100 L Street, N.W.
Washington, D.C. 20037

I f you are planning a trip and you share your life with a pet, you have a few decisions to make before you set off. The following are some tips to help you plan a safer and smoother trip for both you and your pet.

SHOULD YOU TRAVEL WITH YOUR PET?

Some pets are not suited for travel because of temperament, illness or physical impairment. If you have any doubts about whether it is appropriate for your pet to travel, talk to your veterinarian.

If you decide that your pet should not travel with you, consider the alternatives: have a responsible friend or relative look after your pet, board your pet at a kennel or hire a sitter to visit, feed and exercise your pet.

If a friend or relative is going to take care of your pet, ask if that person can take your pet into his or her home. Animals can get lonely when left at home alone. Be sure that your pet is comfortable with his or her temporary caretaker and any pets that person has.

If you choose to board your pet, get references and inspect the kennel Your veterinarian or local shelter can help you select a facility. If you are hiring a sitter, interview the candidates and check their references. (A pet sitter may be preferable if your pet is timid or elderly and needs the comfort of familiar surroundings during your absence.)

Whatever option you choose, there are a few things to remember. Your pet should be up to date on all vaccinations and in sound health. Whoever is caring for your pet should know the telephone number at which you can be reached, the name and telephone number of your veterinarian, and your pet's medical or dietary needs. Be sure that your pet is comfortable with the person you have chosen to take care of him or her.

If You Plan to Travel With Your Pet

THE PRE-TRIP VETERINARY EXAMINATION

Before any trip, have your veterinarian examine your pet to ensure that he or she is in good health. A veterinary examination is a requisite for obtaining the legal documents required for many forms of travel.

In addition to the examination, your veterinarian should provide necessary vaccinations such as rabies, distemper, infectious hepatitis and leptospirosis. If your pet is already up to date on these, obtain written proof.

Your veterinarian may prescribe a tranquilizer for the pet who is a nervous traveler; however, such drugs should be considered only after discussion with your veterinarian. He or she may recommend a trial run in which your pet is given the prescribed dosage and you can observe the effects. Do not give your pet any drug not prescribed or given to you by your veterinarian.

LEGAL REQUIREMENTS

When traveling with your pet, it is always advisable to keep a health certificate (a document from your veterinarian certifying that your pet is in good health) and medical records close at hand. If you and your pet will be traveling across state lines, you must obtain from your veterinarian a certificate of rabies vaccination.

Although pets may travel freely throughout the United States as long as they have proper documentation, Hawaii requires a 120-day quarantine for all dogs and cats. Hawaii's quarantine regulations vary by species, so check prior to travel.

If you and your pet are traveling from the United States to Canada, you must carry a certificate issued by a veterinarian that clearly identifies the animal and certifies that the dog or cat has been vaccinated against rabies during the preceding thirty-six-month period. Different Canadian provinces may have different requirements. Be sure to contact the government of the province you plan to visit.

If you and your pet are traveling to Mexico, you must carry a health certificate prepared by your veterinarian within two weeks of the day you cross the border. The certificate must include a description of your pet, the lot number of the rabies vaccine used, indication of distemper vaccination and a veterinarian's statement that the animal is free from infectious or contagious disease. This certificate must be stamped by an office of the U.S. Department of Agriculture (USDA). The fee for the stamp is $4.

Get Ready to Hit the Road

TRAVEL CARRIERS

Travel carriers are useful when your pet is traveling by car; they are mandatory when your pet is traveling by air. Your pet's carrier should be durable and smooth-edged with opaque sides, a grille door, and several ventilation holes on each of the four sides. Choose a carrier with a secure door and door latch. If you are traveling by air, your carrier should have food and water dishes. Pet carriers may be purchased from pet-supply stores or bought directly from domestic airlines. Select a carrier that has enough room to permit your animal to sit and lie down, but is not large enough to allow your pet to be tossed about during travel. You can make the carrier more comfortable by lining the interior with shredded newspaper or a towel. (For air-travel requirements, see the "Traveling by Air" section.)

It is wise to acclimate your pet to the carrier in the months or weeks preceding your trip. Permit your pet to explore the carrier. Place your pet's food dish inside the carrier and confine him or her to the carrier for brief periods.

To introduce your pet to car travel in the carrier, confine him or her in the carrier and take short drives around the neighborhood. If properly introduced to car travel, most dogs and cats will quickly adjust to and even enjoy car trips.

CAREFUL PREPARATION IS KEY

When packing, don't forget your pet's food, food and water dishes, bedding, litter and litter box, leash, collar and tags, grooming supplies, a first-aid kit and any necessary medications. Always have a container of drinking water with you.

Your pet should wear a sturdy collar with I.D. tags throughout the trip. The tags should have both your permanent address and telephone number and an address and telephone number where you or a contact can be reached during your travels.

Traveling can be upsetting to your pet's stomach. Take along ice cubes, which are easier on your pet than large amounts of water. You should keep feeding to a minimum during travel. (Provide a light meal for your pet two or three hours before you leave, if you are traveling by car, or four to six hours before departure, if you are traveling by airplane.) Allow small amounts of water periodically in the hours before the trip.

On Your Way

TRAVELING BY CAR

Dogs who enjoy car travel need not be confined to a carrier if your car has a restraining harness (available at pet-supply stores) or if you are accompanied by a passenger who can restrain the dog. Because most cats are not as comfortable traveling in cars, for their own safety as well as yours, it is best to keep them in a carrier.

Dogs and cats should always be kept safely inside the car. Pets who are allowed to stick their heads out the window can be injured by particles of debris or become ill from having cold air forced into their lungs. Never transport a pet in the back of an open pickup truck.

Stop frequently to allow your pet to exercise and eliminate. Never permit your pet to leave the car without a collar, I.D. tag and leash.

Never leave your pet unattended in a parked car. On warm days, the temperature in your car can rise to 160°F in a matter of minutes, even with the windows opened slightly. Furthermore, an animal left alone in a car is an open invitation to pet thieves.

TRAVELING BY AIR

Although thousands of pets fly without experiencing problems every year, there are still risks involved. The HSUS recommends that you do not transport your pet by air unless absolutely necessary.

If you must transport your companion animal by air, call the airline to check health and immunization requirements for your pet.

If your pet is a cat or a small dog, take him or her on board with you. Be sure to contact airlines to find out the specific requirements for this option. If you pursue this option, you have two choices: airlines will accept either hard-sided carriers or soft-sided carriers, which may be more comfortable for your pet. Only certain brands of soft-sided carriers are acceptable to certain airlines, so call your airline to find out what carrier to use.

If your pet must travel in the cargo hold, you can increase the chances of a safe flight for your pet by following these tips:

- Use direct flights. You will avoid the mistakes that occur during airline transfers and possible delays in getting your pet off the plane.

- Always travel on the same flight as your pet. Ask the airline if you can watch your pet being loaded into and unloaded from the cargo hold.

- When you board the plane, notify the captain and at least one flight attendant that your pet is traveling in the cargo hold. If the captain knows that pets are on board, he or she may take special precautions.

- Do not ship pug-nosed dogs and cats (such as Pekingese, Chow Chows and Persians) in the cargo hold. These breeds have short nasal passages that leave them vulnerable to oxygen deprivation and heat stroke in cargo holds.

- If traveling during the summer or winter months, choose flights that will accommodate the temperature extremes: early morning or late evening flights are better in the summer; afternoon flights are better in the winter.

- Fit your pet with two pieces of identification — a permanent I.D. tag with your name, home address and telephone number, and a temporary travel I.D. with the address and telephone number where you or a contact person can be reached.

- Affix a travel label to the carrier, stating your name, permanent address and telephone number, and final destination. The label should clearly state where you or a contact person can be reached as soon as the flight arrives.

- Make sure that your pet's nails have been clipped to protect against their hooking in the carrier's door, holes and other crevices.

- Give your pet at least a month before your flight to become familiar with the travel carrier. This will minimize his or her stress during travel.

- Your pet should not be given tranquilizers unless they are prescribed by your veterinarian. Make sure your veterinarian understands that this prescription is for air travel.

- Do not feed your pet for four to six hours prior to air travel. Small amounts of water can be given before the trip. If possible, put ice cubes in the water tray attached to the inside of your pet's kennel. A full water bowl will only spill and cause discomfort.

- Try not to fly with your pet during busy travel times such as holidays and summer. Your pet is more likely to undergo rough handling during hectic travel periods.

- Carry a current photo of your pet with you. If your pet is lost during the trip, a photograph will make it easier for airline employees to search effectively.

- When you arrive at your destination, open the carrier as soon as you are in a safe place and examine your pet. If anything seems wrong, take your pet to a veterinarian immediately. Get the results of the examination in writing, including the date and time.

Do not hesitate to complain if you witness the mishandling of an animal — either yours or someone else's — at any airport.

    If you have a bad experience when shipping your animal by air, contact The HSUS, the U.S. Department of Agriculture (USDA), and the airline involved. To contact the USDA write to USDA, Animal, Plant and Health Inspection Service (APHIS), Washington, D.C. 20250.

TRAVELING BY SHIP

With the exception of assistance dogs, only a few cruise lines accept pets — normally only on ocean crossings and frequently confined to kennels. Some lines permit pets in private cabins. Contact cruise lines in advance to find out their policies and which of their ships have kennel facilities. If you must use the ship's kennel, make sure it is protected from the elements.

Follow the general guidelines suggested for other modes of travel when planning a ship voyage.

TRAVELING BY TRAIN

Amtrak currently does not accept pets for transport unless they are assistance dogs. (There may be smaller U.S. railroad companies that permit animals on board their trains.) Many trains in European countries allow pets. Generally, it is the passengers' responsibility to feed and exercise their pets at station stops.

HOTEL ACCOMMODATIONS

There are approximately eight thousand hotels, motels and inns across the United States that accept guests with pets. Most hotels set their own policies, so it is important to call ahead and ask if pets are permitted and if there is a size limit.

IF YOUR PET IS LOST

Whenever you travel with your pet, there is a chance that you and your pet will become separated. It only takes a moment for an animal to stray and become lost. If your pet is missing, immediately canvass the area. Should your pet not be located within a few hours, take the following actions:

- Contact the animal control departments and humane societies within a sixty-mile radius of where your pet strayed. Check with them each day.

- Post signs at intersections and in storefronts throughout the area.

- Provide a description and a photograph of your missing pet to the police, letter carriers or delivery people.

- Advertise in newspapers and with radio stations. Be certain to list your hotel telephone number on all lost-pet advertisements.

A lost pet may become confused and wary of strangers. Therefore, it may be days or even weeks before the animal is retrieved by a Good Samaritan. If you must continue on your trip or return home, arrange for a hotel clerk or shelter employee to contact you if your pet is located.

DO YOUR PART TO MAKE PETS WELCOME GUESTS

Many hotels, restaurants and individuals will give your pet special consideration during your travels. It is important for you to do your part to ensure that dogs and cats will continue to be welcomed as traveling companions. Obey local animal-control ordinances, keep your animal under restraint, be thoughtful and courteous to other travelers and have a good trip!

If you have more specific questions or are traveling with a companion animal other than a dog or cat, contact the Companion Animals section of The HSUS.

HELPFUL HINTS

- To transport birds out of the United States, record the leg-band or tattoo number on the USDA certificate and get required permits from the U.S Fish and Wildlife Service.

- Carry a current photograph of your pet with you. If your pet is lost during a trip, a photograph will make it easier for others (airline employees, the police, shelter workers, etc.) to help find your pet.

- While thousands of pets fly without problems every year, there are risks involved. The HSUS recommends that you do not transport your pet by air unless absolutely necessary.

- Whenever you travel with your pet, there is a chance that you and your pet will be separated. If your pet is lost, immediately canvass the area and take appropriate action.

Things You Should Know Before Traveling To Canada

HEALTH CERTIFICATES

When traveling with a pet to Canada you must have a health certificate signed by a licensed veterinarian. The certificate will validate when the last vaccinations were given. If your pet's vaccinations are due to expire while you are on vacation, you will want to bring their vaccinations up to date. You will need to present this certificate when leaving and re-entering the United States. If you have a puppy or kitten that is too young to be vaccinated, or a pet that does not require vaccinations, such as a bird, a health certificate will testify to that and assure the health and condition of your pet. (See "Traveling With Your Pet" by the Humane Society of the United States for further information.)

PROOF OF CITIZENSHIP AND PASSPORTS

Passports are not required for citizens of the United States traveling to Canada. However, proof of citizenship in the form of either a baptismal certificate, birth certificate or voter's certificate are necessary. Naturalized citizens will need to carry their papers. Alien Registration Cards are required for aliens residing in the United States. If a minor child is traveling with you, in addition to proof of citizenship, you must present a notarized letter of consent signed by both parents or guardians.

PERSONAL BAGGAGE AND POSSESSIONS

Baggage may be brought into Canada without payment of taxes or duty on a temporary basis only. Occasionally a refundable security deposit may be required by Customs. Your bags may include clothing, personal effects, sporting goods, cameras, food products and other items appropriate for the length of your stay. All items brought into the country must accompany you upon departure.

There are some limitations on tobacco and alcohol. Only 50 cigars, 200 cigarettes or 14 ounces of tobacco is allowed per person. Alcoholic beverages are limited to 300 ounces of beer or ale, equivalent to 24 bottles or cans, or 40 ounces of liquor or wine. You must be in the country for a minimum of 24 hours. Federal duty and taxes may be added to amounts of alcohol or tobacco exceeding these limits.

MEDICATIONS FOR YOU AND YOUR PET

If either you or your pet are required to take medicines that contain narcotics or other habit-forming drugs, carry only the quantities you will normally use during the time you are visiting Canada. Keep medications in their original, properly identified containers. It is always a good idea to carry a written statement from your physician affirming that you are under a doctor's care and require these prescriptions. Your pet's health certificate will note any medications required.

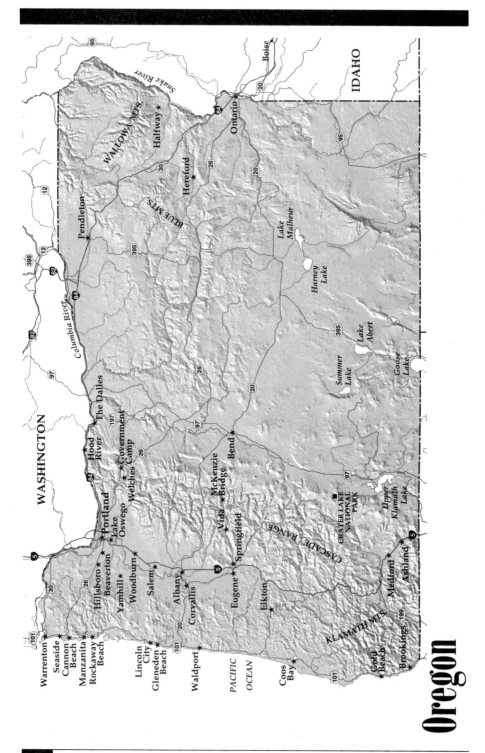

Oregon

Pacific Northwest – Oregon

Albany –
Pony Soldier Inn...21

Ashland –
Windmill's Ashland Hills Inn and Suites...22

Beaverton –
Greenwood Inn...23

Bend –
Red Lion Inn – Bend North...24
Riverhouse Resort...25

Brookings –
Sea Dreamer Inn...26

Cannon Beach –
Ecola Creek Lodge...27
Hallmark Resort...28
Surfsand Resort...29

Coos Bay –
Coos Bay Manor...30

Corvallis –
Ashwood Bed and Breakfast...31

Elkton –
Big K Guest Ranch...32

Eugene –
New Oregon Motel – Best Western...33
Valley River Inn...34

Gleneden Beach –
Salishan Lodge...35

Gold Beach –
Jot's Resort...36
Sand 'n Sea Motel...37

Government Camp –
Mount Hood Inn...38

Halfway –
Pine Valley Lodge...39

Hereford –
Fort Reading Bed and Breakfast...40

Hillsboro –
Hallmark Inn – Best Western...41

Hood River –
Columbia Gorge Hotel...42
Hood River Hotel...43

Lake Oswego –
Crowne Plaza Hotel...44

Lincoln City –
Sea Horse Oceanfront Lodging...45

Manzanita –
Sunset Vacation Rentals...46

McKenzie Bridge –
Country Place...47

Medford –
Shilo Inn...48

Mill City –
Morrison Cottage...49

Ontario –
Best Western Inn...50

Pendleton -
DoubleTree Hotel...51

Portland –
Benson Hotel...52
Fifth Avenue Suites Hotel...53
Hotel Vintage Plaza...54
Marriott Downtown...55
River Place Hotel...56

Rockaway Beach –

Ocean Locomotion on the Beach...57

Salem –

Phoenix Inn...58

Seaside –

Comfort Inn – Boardwalk...59

Ocean View Resort – Best Western...60

Springfield –

DoubleTree Hotel – Eugene-Springfield...61

Rodeway Inn...62

The Dalles –

Quality Inn...63

Vida –

Wayfarer Resort...64

Waldport –

Edgewater Cottages...65

Warrenton –

Shilo Inn...66

Welches –

Old Welches Inn Bed and Breakfast...67

Woodburn –

Holiday Inn Express...68

Yamhill –

Flying M Ranch...69

Pony Soldier Inn

Pony Soldier Inn
315 Airport Road Southeast
Albany, Oregon 97321
800-634-PONY • (541) 928-6322

Room Rates:	$72 – $83, including continental breakfast. AARP discount.
Pet Charges or Deposits:	None. Manager's approval required. Small pets only.
Rated: 3 Paws 🐾🐾🐾	72 guest rooms with refrigerators, heated swimming pool, whirlpool, exercise room and laundry facilities.

The Pony Soldier Inn is a convenient, affordable and comfortable choice, offering a full acre of lovely landscaped grounds specifically for your pet's needs.

Historic Albany is known for antique shopping, touring the many area wineries and photographing the covered bridges. There are also self-guided driving tours throughout the city's historic areas, with opportunities to view splendid Victorian homes. This historic town highlights Queen Anne, Italianate, French Second Empire and Classic Revival styles of architecture.

Windmill's Ashland Hills Inn and Suites

Windmill's Ashland Hills Inn and Suites
2525 Ashland Street
Ashland, Oregon 97520
800-547-4747 • (541) 482-8310

Room Rates:	$46 – $250, including continental or full breakfast.
Pet Charges or Deposits:	None.
Rated: 4 Paws 🐾 🐾 🐾 🐾	145 guest rooms and 85 luxury suites, some with kitchens, seasonal outdoor swimming pool and whirlpool, fitness room, tennis courts, laundry facilities, jogging path, bicycles, helicopter landing pad, restaurant and lounge.

N estled in the foothills of Southern Oregon's Cascade Mountains, in the famed town of Ashland, is Windmill's Ashland Hills Inn and Suites, one of the Northwest's premier resort destinations. Whether you choose one of the comfortable guest rooms with a panoramic view of the Cascade Mountains, or a spacious two-bedroom suite, all guests receive the same attention to detail and excellent service.

Your day begins with complimentary morning coffee, juice, muffins and the morning newspaper delivered to your door. For your recreational pleasure, the Inn has a seasonal heated swimming pool and whirlpool, a fitness room, tennis courts, a jogging path, bicycles for guests to enjoy and beautifully landscaped, spacious grounds for you and your pet to explore.

The influence of the theater and arts can be seen throughout the town. The area also offers horseback riding, river rafting on the Rogue or Klamath rivers and salmon, steelhead or trout fishing. Ashland also has many award-winning wineries and several nearby golf courses and parks for you to enjoy.

Greenwood Inn

Greenwood Inn
10700 Southwest Allen Boulevard
Beaverton, Oregon 97005
800-289-1300 • (803) 643-7444

Room Rates:	$87 – $148, including continental breakfast.
Pet Charges or Deposits:	$10 per day. $100 refundable deposit.
Rated: 4 Paws 🐾🐾🐾🐾	250 guest rooms and 26 suites, some with kitchens, decks, fireplaces and private whirlpools; 2 heated swimming pools, sauna, whirlpool, exercise room, restaurant and cocktail lounge.

From the lush landscaping to the inviting Northwest architecture — every detail welcomes you to the Greenwood Inn. Clearly, your comfort is their first consideration here, with custom furnishings, refrigerators, tasteful prints and original Northwest art. Oversized work stations, two-line phones and computer hook-up capabilities appeal to the professional.

Unexpected touches include guest shuttles to nearby business parks, shopping and local attractions, use of a local athletic club and the on-site exercise room, two outdoor pools and Jacuzzi.

Red Lion Inn – Bend North

Red Lion Inn – Bend North
1415 Northeast Third Street
Bend, Oregon 97701
800-RED-LION • (541) 382-7011

Room Rates:	$52 – $94. AAA and AARP discounts.
Pet Charges or Deposits:	None.
Rated: 3 Paws 🐾 🐾 🐾	75 guest rooms and 2 family suites, outdoor swimming pool, spa, 2 saunas, room service, laundry, restaurant and cocktail lounge.

L ocated in scenic Central Oregon, near Mount Bachelor and the Deschutes National Forest, is the Red Lion Inn offering completely remodeled guest rooms and family suites.

Recreation facilities include an outdoor swimming pool and spa as well as two private saunas. Golf, river-rafting, fishing and skiing at Mount Bachelor are all nearby.

Bend offers a wide selection of restaurants, coffee shops and microbreweries sure to satisfy any whim of the culinary imagination.

Riverhouse Resort

Riverhouse Resort
3075 North Highway 97
Bend, Oregon 97701
800-547-3928 • (541) 389-3111

Room Rates:	$57 – $175. Packages available.
Pet Charges or Deposits:	None.
Rated: 4 Paws	220 guest rooms and suites, indoor and outdoor heated pools, spa, sauna, exercise room, jogging trails, golf course, restaurants, entertainment and dancing.

L ocated on the banks of the picturesque Deschutes River is the Riverhouse Resort, offering guests a wide selection of room accommodations that include kitchens, fireplaces and spa tubs.

Relax in the saunas and heated whirlpool, stay with shape with the exercise room and indoor pool or enjoy a scenic jog along the river. The Riverhouse even has a championship golf course, River's Edge, open year-round.

With three restaurants on the property and others nearby, you have a wide variety of dining choices. After dinner, enjoy some the Northwest's finest entertainment in the popular Fireside Nightclub.

Sea Dreamer Inn

Sea Dreamer Inn
15167 McVay Lane
Brookings, Oregon 97415
800-408-4367 • (541) 469-6629

Room Rates:	$50 – $80, including full breakfast.
Pet Charges or Deposits:	$10 per stay. Call for deposit requirements. Manager's approval required.
Rated: 3 Paws	4 guest rooms, two with private baths, two with shared baths.

Built of redwood in 1912, this country Victorian commands a view of Southern Oregon's famous lily fields, gently sloping to the ocean. The oldest home of its kind in Curry County, the Sea Dreamer Inn is surrounded by spacious grounds amidst pine, fruit trees and flowers that bloom year-round.

Awaken to the smell of fresh coffee and baking breads. Breakfast is served in the Inn's formal dining room. You will enjoy magnificent sunsets and whale-watching from the front porch. There is a warm, cozy fire for those chilly nights and rainy winter days.

Ecola Creek Lodge

Ecola Creek Lodge
P.O. Box 1040
Cannon Beach, Oregon 97110
800-873-2749 • (503) 436-2776

Room Rates:	$70 – $170, including continental breakfast. Call for discounts.
Pet Charges or Deposits:	$10 per day. Sorry, no cats.
Rated: 3 Paws 🐾 🐾 🐾	10 unique guest rooms and 10 spacious suites with fireplaces, living rooms and kitchens.

ne of Cannon Beach's most recognizable landmarks, the Lodge consists of four Cape Cod-style buildings with stained glass, spacious lawns, fountains, flower gardens and a lily pond.

No two rooms are alike. The rooms are furnished with art from the Oregon Gallery and they range from individual guest rooms to two-bedroom suites that can accommodate up to a family of seven.

Tucked away in the quaint village of Cannon Beach, on a four-mile strip between the mountainous coastal range and the Pacific Ocean, Ecola Creek Lodge sits back from the ocean about 600 yards. There are no buildings between the Lodge and the ocean, only Ecola State Park and Ecola Creek.

The abundance of natural beauty in and around the village explains why it has become a gathering place for artists. The area is blessed with exceptional ecological beauty, wide sandy beaches and towering basalt rocks.

Hallmark Resort

Hallmark Resort
1400 South Hemlock
Cannon Beach, Oregon 97100
888-448-4449 • 800-345-5676 • (503) 436-1566
Web Site: www.hallmarkinns.com

Room Rates:	$59 – $229. AAA, AARP, AKC and ABA discounts.
Pet Charges or Deposits:	$8 per day. Limit 2 pets.
Rated: 4 Paws 🐾🐾🐾🐾	132 rooms and suites, fireplaces, ocean views, fully equipped kitchens, spa units, recreation center with heated pool, wading pool, two swirl spas, dry sauna and exercise room.

O verlooking the famous Haystack Rock and the majestic Pacific Ocean, the Hallmark Resort commands dramatic views of the Northwest coastline. Located at the base of the coastal mountain range, Cannon Beach is blessed with a dramatic shoreline and moderate climate.

Guest accommodations range from cozy rooms for two to luxurious two-bedroom suites with fully equipped kitchens, designed for a family of six. Most rooms include a gas fireplace and spacious deck.

Relax or work out in the indoor recreation center, complete with heated pool, two whirlpool spas, dry sauna and exercise room. Things to see and do and experience are nearly endless in the Cannon Beach area. Take a leisurely stroll on seven miles of pristine beach and maybe even build a sand castle or two.

Surfsand Resort

Surfsand Resort
P.O. Box 219
Cannon Beach, Oregon 97110
800-547-6100 • (503) 436-2274
Web Site: www.surfsand.com
E-mail: surfsand@transport.com

Room Rates:	$109 – $299. AARP discount.
Pet Charges or Deposits:	$5 per pet, per day.
Rated: 3 Paws	53 oceanfront guest rooms and 27 suites, fireplaces and whirlpools, heated indoor pool, health club privileges, laundry facilities, restaurant and cocktail lounge.

A t the Surfsand Resort, every effort has been made to accommodate the entire family, including pets. This oceanfront property, just steps from the famous Haystack Rock, features room styles as varied as those who visit.

You'll find everything from spacious suites to studios, many with Jacuzzi tubs, wet bars and fully stocked kitchens, in addition to fireplaces, private balconies and breathtaking views of the Pacific Ocean.

Whether hiking miles of scenic trails, jogging or biking on the sandy beach, swimming laps in the indoor pool or using your free passes to the Cannon Beach Athletic Club, there's something for everyone here.

Coos Bay Manor

Coos Bay Manor
955 South 5th Street
Coos Bay, Oregon 97420
800-269-1224 • (541) 269-1224

Room Rates:	$65 – $100, including full breakfast. AARP discount.
Pet Charges or Deposits:	$10 per stay.
Rated: 3 Paws	5 rooms, 3 with private baths.

Built in 1912, the historic Colonial-style Coos Bay Manor offers guests their choice of five charming, individually decorated rooms. The house has a unique open-air balcony that surrounds the second floor, detailed woodworking throughout and large rooms with high ceilings.

The Victorian Room is full of lace, ruffles, romance and elegance, featuring a sitting area overlooking the rolling hills. An Old West theme and a queen-sized feather bed are enjoyed in the Cattle Baron's Room. The Country Room is old-fashioned, warm and inviting, just like Grandma's house, with a brass queen-sized bed and handmade quilts.

Each morning a full gourmet breakfast is served in the dining room.

Ashwood Bed and Breakfast

Ashwood Bed and Breakfast
2940 Northwest Ashwood Drive
Corvallis, Oregon 97330-1256
800-306-5136 • (541) 757-9772
Web Site: www.moriah.com/ashwood
E-mail: ashwood@proaxis.com

Room Rates:	$60 – $70, including full breakfast.
Pet Charges or Deposits:	$10 per stay, $10 refundable deposit. Manager's approval required.
Rated: 3 Paws 🐾 🐾 🐾	3 guest rooms, landscaped yard, guest privileges at nearby athletic club.

I n an oak forest set in a quiet neighborhood of northwest Corvallis is the family-style Ashwood Bed and Breakfast Inn. Conveniently located near Oregon State University, guests can walk to shopping, restaurants and the Timberhill Athletic Club, where they can work out compliments of the Inn.

Although there are only three guest rooms, visitors are encouraged to make use of the living room area and the screened patio with its fenced yard. The resident pets, Dancer the basset hound and Diego the tabby cat, will gladly show your pets all the best places in the area to explore.

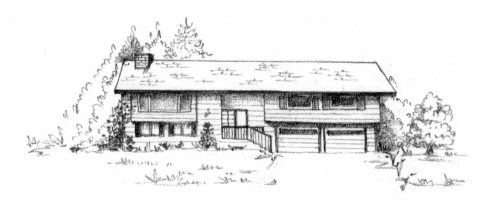

Big K Guest Ranch

Big K Guest Ranch
20029 Highway 138 West
Elkton, Oregon 97436
800-390-2445 • (541) 584-2295

Room Rates:	$195 – $250, including all meals.
Pet Charges or Deposits:	$10 per day. Manager's approval required.
Rated: 4 Paws 🐾🐾🐾🐾	20 private cabins, some suites with fireplaces and Jacuzzis, game room, exercise room, fly-casting pond, fishing excursions, skeet-shooting, horseshoes, scenic river float trips, bicycle rentals, picnic facilities, horseback riding and hiking trails.

T his working ranch is set on 2,500 remote, wooded acres along the 10-mile scenic Umpqua River. Guests may choose from 20 spacious country pine cabins with fireplaces and Jacuzzis. Home-style dining, in this unique country atmosphere, is included in the price of your room.

Professional guides are available to escort you along the Umpqua, to angle for salmon, steelhead, smallmouth bass and shad. Trail rides and hiking treks take you through meadows and forests of tall conifers and oaks to view deer, elk, turkey, osprey and eagles.

New Oregon Motel – Best Western

New Oregon Motel – Best Western
1655 Franklin Boulevard
Eugene, Oregon 97403
800-528-1234 • (541) 683-3669
E-mail: neworegon@aol.com

Room Rates:	$55 – $85. AAA discount.
Pet Charges or Deposits:	$25 refundable deposit.
Rated: 3 Paws 🐾 🐾 🐾	128 rooms and 8 family suites, indoor pool, saunas, Jacuzzi, racquetball and fitness center, refrigerator, laundry facilities, restaurant, bar and bistro.

A djacent to the University of Oregon campus and downtown Eugene, overlooking the Willamette River, is the New Oregon Motel – Best Western. The spacious guest rooms and two-bedroom family suites offer you conveniences such as an in-room refrigerator and 24-hour laundry facilities.

The sports complex, located across from the lobby, features racquetball, weight and aerobic equipment, a sauna and an indoor swimming pool. For an outdoor workout, the Willamette River jogging trails are located alongside the property.

Valley River Inn

Valley River Inn
1000 Valley River Way
P.O. Box 10088
Eugene, Oregon 97401
800-543-8266 • (541) 687-0123

Room Rates:	$135 – $300; special family amenities.
Pet Charges or Deposits:	None. Complimentary pet packs.
Rated: 4 Paws 🐾🐾🐾🐾	248 guest rooms and 9 suites, many with balconies; swimming pool, saunas, whirlpool, jogging path, bicycles, restaurant and lounge.

With so much to see and do, it's nice to come home to the casual elegance of the Valley River Inn's towering wooden beams, brick and copper fireplaces and spacious rooms and suites. Perched on the lush banks of the Willamette River, this Mobil Four-Star hotel offers all the amenities you would expect from any upscale resort.

Your pet will appreciate the complimentary "Pet Pack," which includes a toy, a bone and directions to local pet stores, parks and veterinary hospitals.

Sweetwaters Restaurant and Lounge serves Pacific Northwest cuisine, created from fresh seasonal ingredients and locally grown foods. Sunday brunch is a must.

Salishan Lodge

Salishan Lodge
7760 North Highway 101
Gleneden Beach, Oregon 97388
800-452-2300 • (541) 764-2371
Web Site: www.dolce.com

Room Rates:	$135 – $279. AAA and AARP discounts.
Pet Charges or Deposits:	$15 per day.
Rated: 5 Paws 🐾🐾🐾🐾🐾	205 guest rooms and 3 luxury suites, many with fireplaces and balconies with ocean or forest views, nature trails, putting green and 18-hole golf course, tennis club, beach, heated indoor pool, saunas, whirlpool, massage, wine cellar and restaurant.

An acclaimed and treasured hideaway of the Pacific Northwest, Salishan is quietly woven into Mother Nature's spectacular surroundings. You will immediately feel at one with Salishan – just steps from the mountains and sea, gently tucked into this secluded setting.

Guest rooms are native wood structures of pine and cedar, built in harmony with the naturally landscaped surroundings, and decorated with original Northwest art. Most rooms include a fireplace and private balcony overlooking the forest, links or bay. Treat yourself to a fireside massage in the privacy of your room.

Vegetables from area market gardeners, hook-and-line caught fish from local day boats, and shellfish raised and harvested in nearby bays are prepared and flavored in a tempting Pacific Northwest cuisine at Salishan Lodge.

Jot's Resort

Jot's Resort
94360 Wedderburn Loop Road
P.O. Box J
Gold Beach, Oregon 97444
800-367-5687 • (541) 247-6676
Web Site: www.jotsresort.com

Room Rates:	$85 – $295. AAA and AARP discounts.
Pet Charges or Deposits:	$10 per pet, per day. Manager's approval required.
Rated: 3 Paws 🐾 🐾 🐾	140 standard, deluxe and family units, spacious suites and condos with water views, some efficiencies and kitchens, balconies, indoor and outdoor swimming pools, sauna, whirlpool, fitness room, marina, boat and bicycle rentals, restaurant and cocktail lounge.

A t Jot's Resort, the Pacific Ocean and the Rogue River meet to create unique recreational opportunities for the whole family, from crabbing, clam-digging, tide-pooling, boating, biking, beachcombing, trail riding, swimming, wind-surfing, deep-sea fishing and year-round salmon and steelhead angling on the legendary Rogue.

Choose from one of the many waterfront units with views of the river, private sun decks, full kitchens and fireplaces.

Sand 'n Sea Motel

Sand 'n Sea Motel
29362 Ellensburg Avenue
Gold Beach, Oregon 97444
800-808-SAND • (541) 247-6658

Room Rates:	$40 – $100.
Pet Charges or Deposits:	$5 per pet, per day.
Rated: 3 Paws	43 guest rooms and suites, fireplaces, ocean views, private balconies or patios, spa and exercise facilities plus a separate A-frame cabin on the beach.

O n a knoll overlooking a sandy beach on the scenic Southern Oregon coast is the Sand 'n Sea. Private beach frontage allows guests unlimited opportunity to enjoy the best the ocean has to offer.

Here you will find oceanfront rooms with private balconies or patios to enjoy spectacular sunsets, or an A-frame cabin that sits directly on the beach.

Gold Beach is home of the famous Rogue River, with its world-class fishing and jet-boat excursions. Harbor seals, otters and osprey are just a few of the abundant wildlife species visible along the banks of the Rogue.

Mount Hood Inn

Mount Hood Inn
87450 East Government Camp Loop
P.O. Box 400
Government Camp, Oregon 97028
800-443-7777 • (503) 272-3205

Room Rates:	$125 – $155, including continental breakfast. AAA and AARP discounts. Ski packages available.
Pet Charges or Deposits:	$5 per day.
Rated: 3 Paws 🐾 🐾 🐾	56 guest rooms, some with whirlpools and refrigerators, heated swimming pool, large indoor spa, laundry facilities, complimentary ski lockers and ski toning room.

I n the village of Government Camp in Mount Hood National Park is the Mount Hood Inn. Conveniently located within minutes of Timberline Ski Area, Mount Hood Meadows and Skibowl, the inn is a favorite for visitors and locals year-round. The modern guest rooms offer spectacular views of the surrounding mountains.

In Mount Hood National Forest, you will discover rambling streams and remote lakes to fish, horseback riding, mountain biking and several scenic trails to explore with your dog.

Pine Valley Lodge

Pine Valley Lodge
163 North Main Street
P.O. Box 712
Halfway, Oregon 97834
(541) 742-2027

Room Rates:	$65 – $105, including full breakfast.
Pet Charges or Deposits:	None.
Rated: 3 Paws 🐾 🐾 🐾	4 rooms and 2 suites.

D irectly across the street from the Olde Church, the Pine Valley Lodge is surrounded by porches to lounge and relax on. The large Great Room is homelike, with numerous games to enjoy or room to curl up and read a good book from the library. The lodge features artistically appointed accommodations with eiderdown comforters, fine linens and comfortable beds.

This eclectic hideaway offers elegant frontier dining in a whimsical country setting, reminiscent of the Old West. The creations that emanate from Babette's kitchen represent, perhaps, the supreme art form practiced by your multitalented hosts. Hand-crafted European breads, pastries, even real, chewy New York bagels are baked on the premises. A pot of great soup is always on and something to go with it — and espresso, too.

Fort Reading Bed and Breakfast

Fort Reading Bed and Breakfast
HCR 86 Box 140
Hereford, Oregon 97837
800-573-4285 • (541) 446-3478

Room Rates:	$45 – $75, including full breakfast.
Pet Charges or Deposits:	Half the room rate as deposit. Manager's approval required.
Rated: 3 Paws 🐾 🐾 🐾	A rustic, two-bedroom cabin with full kitchen on a working cattle ranch. Located near state parks, lakes, fishing, hiking and historic sites.

Y ou'll step back in time when you enter this rustic, two-bedroom ranch house adjacent to the main ranch house. Choose from a farm-style breakfast in the cozy ranch kitchen or prepare your own meals in the cabin's full kitchen. Picnic lunches and dinners are available upon request.

The ranch is located two miles west of Unity Lake, where you can enjoy a day of swimming, fishing or boating. History buffs will want to explore the historic mining town of Sumpter, the Oregon Trail Interpretive Center, local museums, old ghost towns and historic cemeteries, all within an hour's drive of Fort Reading Bed and Breakfast.

Hallmark Inn – Best Western

Hallmark Inn – Best Western
3500 Northeast Cornell Road
Hillsboro, Oregon 97124
800-336-3797 • (503) 648-3500

Room Rates:	$74 – $125, including continental breakfast. AAA and AARP discounts.
Pet Charges or Deposits:	$5 per day, plus $75 refundable deposit.
Rated: 4 Paws 🐾🐾🐾🐾	123 guest rooms and 9 suites, refrigerators, microwaves heated swimming pool, whirlpool, exercise room, laundry facilities, restaurant and lounge.

L ocated twenty minutes west of Portland, the town of Hillsboro is nestled in the Tualatin Valley, halfway between the Cascade Mountains and the Pacific Ocean. This area produces thousands of gallons of berry wine and fruit wine annually. You will find numerous guided wine tours and tasting rooms throughout the region.

The appealing theme decor suites of the Hallmark Inn – Best Western offer you quality amenities to make you feel at home. Arise each morning to a complimentary continental breakfast that can be enjoyed on the landscaped grounds or poolside. There is even an exercise room available for guests so you won't miss your daily workout.

Columbia Gorge Hotel

Columbia Gorge Hotel
4000 Westcliff Drive
Hood River, Oregon 97031
800-345-1921 • (541) 386-5566

Room Rates: $150 – $365, including their "World-Famous Farm Breakfast."
Pet Charges or Deposits: $15 per day. "Pet Package" upon check-in.
Rated: 5 Paws 🐾 🐾 🐾 🐾 🐾 42 guest rooms, with river or garden views, fireplaces, award-winning restaurant.

High atop a cliff overlooking the extraordinary Columbia River Gorge is the Columbia Gorge Hotel with its acres of manicured gardens. Built in 1921 by a Portland lumber baron, the hotel has maintained its legendary reputation for hospitality for more than 75 years.

This 11-acre oasis offers a wide selection of distinctive guest rooms. Each features antique furnishings and a view of either the gardens rimming Phelps Creek or the spectacular Columbia River Gorge. The most unique rooms have polished brass or canopy beds, and some of the larger suites have fireplaces. Each evening the turn-down service will leave a fresh rose and sweet chocolate as a final treat for the day.

Upon check-in, four-legged guests will receive a special "Pet Package" consisting of a doggy toy, a chew bone, doggy treats and a special dish with the hotel's logo, to make their stay more enjoyable.

Hood River Hotel

Hood River Hotel
102 Oak Avenue
Hood River, Oregon 97031
800-386-1859 • (541) 386-1900
Web Site: www.hoodriverhotel.com
E-mail: hrhotel@gorge.net

Room Rates:	$49 – $145, including continental breakfast. AAA and AARP discounts.
Pet Charges or Deposits:	$15. Manager's approval required.
Rated: 4 Paws 🐾 🐾 🐾 🐾	32 guest rooms and 9 suites, Jacuzzi, sauna, exercise facilities, restaurant and cocktails.

S tep back in time as you enter Hood River's vintage hotel, which is listed on the National Register of Historic Places. This fully restored 1913 hotel offers river-view rooms and spacious suites decorated with period reproductions.

A new Jacuzzi, sauna and exercise facility is available for guests, as well as the abundant recreation opportunities in the Hood River area. Enjoy horseback riding, golf at nearby Indian Creek Golf Course and year-round snow-skiing at Mount Hood. The historic district offers a self-guided walking tour of several buildings listed on the National Register.

Crowne Plaza Hotel

Crowne Plaza Hotel
14811 Kruse Oaks Boulevard
Lake Oswego, Oregon 97035
800-2-CROWNE • (503) 624-8400

Room Rates:	$119 – $265. AAA and AARP discounts.
Pet Charges or Deposits:	None.
Rated: 3 Paws	161 guest rooms and 12 suites, some with whirlpool tubs, heated indoor/outdoor pools, sauna, whirlpool, exercise room, restaurant and cocktail lounge.

L ocated seven miles south of downtown Portland, the Crowne Plaza Hotel offers guests well-appointed guest rooms and suites with all the amenities one expects from a fine hotel. Upon check-in you will receive a complimentary pass to a full-service athletic club located within minutes of the hotel.

For those who wish to take advantage of the hotel's facilities, there are both indoor and outdoor swimming pools, a sauna and whirlpool, a wonderful sun deck, plus bicycles and tennis rackets for guests to use. Golf courses and tennis courts and the Mary S. Young State Park, a great place for you and your dog to explore, are all located nearby.

Sea Horse Oceanfront Lodging

Sea Horse Oceanfront Lodging
2039 Northwest Harbor
Lincoln City, Oregon 97367
800-662-2101 • (541) 994-2101

Room Rates:	$55 – $120. AAA, AARP, AKC and ABA discounts.
Pet Charges or Deposits:	$5 per pet, per day.
Rated: 3 Paws	60 guest rooms and 10 suites, some with refrigerators and microwaves; indoor heated swimming pool and oceanview spa.

E scape to the beach in affordable comfort with the accommodations of The Sea Horse Oceanfront Lodging. Perched on a bluff overlooking ten miles of sandy white beaches, the Inn offers guests a variety of accommodations to suit the needs of the family on vacation.

You will enjoy the indoor heated swimming pool and the outdoor spa with its dramatic ocean views as the waves gently roll onto shore. The ten miles of pristine oceanfront offers you the opportunity to comb the beach, grab a piece of driftwood and play fetch with your dog, romp in the waves, or take a romantic stroll along the shore at sunset.

Although the inn is private and secluded, it is only minutes from Lincoln City, a popular oceanfront community with restaurants, shopping areas, golf, whale-watching, river-fishing and ocean-fishing. Be sure to visit Drift Creek, where you will find an example of one of the oldest covered bridges in Oregon.

Sunset Vacation Rentals

Sunset Vacation Rentals
P.O. Box 505
Manzanita, Oregon 97130
800-883-7784 • (503) 368-7969
Web Site: www.doormat.com

Room Rates:	$99 – $250.
Pet Charges or Deposits:	$5 per day. $50 refundable deposit. Manager's approval required.
Rated: 4 Paws 🐾🐾🐾🐾	2- to 4-bedroom vacation homes, sleeping up to 12 guests, many oceanfront or with ocean views, with fully equipped kitchens, cable television and VCR, barbecue, telephone, linens, laundry facilities and supplies, cleaning service upon departure, 24-hour assistance and self check-in.

Most of the vacation homes available through Sunset Vacation Rentals have fully equipped kitchens, a barbecue for cookouts, all your linens, laundry facilities and supplies, as well as 24-hour assistance, self check-in and cleaning service upon departure.

When visiting nearby Rockaway, choose from Elbows, a two-story home with knotty-pine interior and spectacular ocean views, or Chuck's Sunset, an ocean-front cozy cabin that sleeps up to six guests, located along a freshwater creek.

For those heading to Twin Rocks, the Captain's Inn is a spacious, three-bedroom, two-bath home located 100 yards from the beach. Nedonna Beach is home to the Crow's Nest, a cozy beach house for up to six guests, only 80 yards from the beach, or D's Cottage, a cute and cozy cottage-style beach house with fabulous ocean views located in Arch Cape.

Country Place

Country Place
56245 Delta Drive
McKenzie Bridge, Oregon 97413
(541) 822-6008

Room Rates:	$68 – $81.
Pet Charges or Deposits:	None. Manager's approval required.
Rated: 3 Paws 🐾🐾🐾	3 housekeeping cabins with separate bedrooms for two to six guests, with fireplaces and kitchens. Also a 4-bedroom main house for six to 24 guests with two fireplaces, complete kitchen, living room, large meeting room and private pool.

P icture yourself in one of the modern, rustic cabins near 500 feet of rushing, tumbling white water. Cabins feature fireplaces, kitchens and separate bedrooms.

The elegant Dutch Colonial mansion is a perfect choice for family gatherings. It has four bedrooms, two with fireplaces, complete modern kitchen facilities and a living room with massive fireplaces. There is a private pool, a play yard for children, Ping-Pong and pool tables.

Relax and enjoy all that the great outdoors has to offer here, from some of the most beautiful mountain trails and lush green forests, to unparalleled fishing for steelhead, salmon, giant chinook and rainbow trout.

Shilo Inn

Shilo Inn
2111 Biddle Road
Medford, Oregon 97504
800-222-2244 • (541) 770-5151
Web Site: www.shiloinns.com

Room Rates:	$49 – $69, including continental breakfast. AAA and AARP discounts.
Pet Charges or Deposits:	$7 per pet, per day.
Rated: 3 Paws 🐾 🐾 🐾	48 guest rooms, some with refrigerators and microwaves; laundry facilities, spa, sauna and steam room.

In Medford, home of the Rogue River National Forest, you will find the affordable Shilo Inn. Your comfortable accommodations will include amenities such as in-room coffeemakers, refrigerators, microwaves, wet bars and guest laundry facilities. Enjoy your complimentary continental breakfast of fresh fruit, muffins, pastries, hot tea and freshly brewed coffee before heading out for your day.

While in the area, be sure to visit the Rogue River National Forest, which offers acres of parkland to explore with your dog. Here you will find Mount Ashland, the highest point in Oregon's Cascade Range, and the headwaters of the Applegate River in the Siskiyou Mountains. This environment includes conifer forests, open woodlands, rocky ridgetops and many botanical specimens native to the Pacific Northwest.

Morrison Cottage

Morrison Cottage
418 Northwest Alder Street
Mill City, Oregon 97360-2131
800-699-5937 • (503) 897-3371

Room Rates:	$65 – $75, including gourmet breakfast basket.
Pet Charges or Deposits:	None. Manager's approval required.
Rated: 3 Paws	2 guest rooms and a 1-bedroom cottage with fireplace, kitchen and private bath with Jacuzzi for two.

L ocated thirty miles east of Salem on the banks of the Santiam River, the Morrison Cottage offers guests a sample of the magic found in this scenic area.

The private cottage, built in 1929, is complete with a kitchen, private bath and cozy fireplace. You will appreciate the attention to detail devoted to your comfort when you slip between the silk sheets and your head sinks into the down-filled pillows.

All guests are welcomed with a breakfast basket of baked goods, the perfect introduction to a country morning and a taste of the simple life.

Best Western Inn

Best Western Inn
251 Goodfellow Street
Ontario, Oregon 97914
800-828-0364 • (541) 889-2600

Room Rates:	$54 – $86, including continental breakfast. AAA and AARP discounts.
Pet Charges or Deposits:	$75 or credit card as refundable deposit.
Rated: 3 Paws 🐾🐾🐾	44 guest rooms and 17 suites, Jacuzzi and hot tub rooms, some refrigerators and microwaves, heated swimming pool, whirlpool, restaurant and cocktail lounge.

At the Best Western Inn the rooms and suites are the best value you'll find within miles of Ontario. All rooms feature color TV with Showtime, some with Jacuzzi tubs, refrigerators and microwaves. A complimentary continental breakfast is included in your room rate.

The Inn is located within a thousand yards of the Snake River and only minutes from numerous recreation activities. Ontario is the gateway to many scenic areas, such as Lake Owyhee, Brownley Lake, Bully Creek and Mallure Butte, where you will find erosion-sculptured canyons, skirted waterways, red-tinted cliffs and other natural wonders for you and your dog to explore.

DoubleTree Hotel

DoubleTree Hotel
304 Southeast Nye Avenue
Pendleton, Oregon 97801
800-222-TREE • (541) 276-6111
Web Site: www.doubletreehotels.com

Room Rates:	$71 – $81. AAA, AARP, AKC and ABA discounts.
Pet Charges or Deposits:	$20 refundable deposit.
Rated: 4 Paws 🐾🐾🐾🐾	169 guest rooms and 1 luxury suite with whirlpool and wet bar; all rooms with private balconies, heated pool, whirlpool, laundry facilities, health club privileges, restaurant, coffee shop and cocktail lounge.

L ocated midway between Portland and Boise is the DoubleTree Hotel, where you will find spacious guest rooms featuring private balconies with spectacular scenic views of the surrounding hills.

The area offers many historic sites you can tour, such as the Living Heritage Tour, which visits the Umatilla Indian Reservation and the Oregon Trail. There are also tours to the Pendleton Underground, a series of tunnels built by Chinese immigrants in the late 1800s.

Benson Hotel

Benson Hotel
300 Southwest Broadway
Portland, Oregon 97205
888-5-BENSON • (503) 228-2000

Room Rates: $190 – $800.
Pet Charges or Deposits: $50. Small pets only.
Rated: 5 Paws 😺 😺 😺 😺 😺 286 guest rooms and 55 suites with fireplaces and whirlpools,
                          exercise room, health club, restaurant and cocktail lounge.

 urrently listed on the National Register of Historic Places, The Benson Hotel has been a Portland landmark since 1912. From its location in the heart of the city's vibrant downtown, the hotel is convenient to everything Portland has to offer.

The Benson provides modern luxury in a classic setting. Whether you select a Grand Suite with a baby grand piano, fireplace and Jacuzzi, a penthouse with a panoramic view of the city, or a specially appointed elegant guest room, you will appreciate the comfort and ambiance.

No visit to The Benson Hotel is complete without dining at the landmark London Grill and Trader Vic's. The menus and decor of each restaurant have been updated, but the elegant fare, excellent service and superb culinary staff have remained the standard for quality for decades.

Fifth Avenue Suites Hotel

Fifth Avenue Suites Hotel
506 Southwest Washington
Portland, Oregon 97204
800-711-2971 • (503) 222-0001
Web Site: www.5thavenuesuites.com

Room Rates: $145 – $190.
Pet Charges or Deposits: None.
Rated: 5 Paws 🐾 🐾 🐾 🐾 🐾 221 deluxe guest rooms and suites, Aveda spa, restaurant.

C arved out of a 1912 building in downtown Portland that once housed a department store, this 10-story, 221-unit hotel is intimate in spite of its size. A wood- and mirror-trimmed, arcaded passageway gives views into the lobby with its soaring ceiling and tall white pillars.

With its cozy seating arrangements and lamps scattered throughout, the lobby feels like your grandmother's living room — assuming your grandmother had plenty of money and good taste. Complimentary wine-tasting every evening, and coffee, tea and juice in the morning, complete the home-like atmosphere.

All guest rooms are beautifully appointed, light and airy, with curtained sliding French door partitions. Color schemes feature soft apricot carpeting paired with saffron and cream tones. Upholstered pieces are overstuffed and the beds have padded headboards and thick brocade bedspreads.

Hotel Vintage Plaza

Hotel Vintage Plaza
422 Southwest Broadway
Portland, Oregon 97205
800-243-0555 • (503) 228-1212

Room Rates:	$165 – $300, complimentary continental breakfast and evening wine tasting. AAA discount. Weekend rates available.
Pet Charges or Deposits:	None.
Rated: 4 Paws 🐾 🐾 🐾 🐾	107 guest rooms and 30 suites, including 9 two-story townhouse suites, 24-hour room service, restaurant and lounge.

C entrally located in the heart of downtown Portland, the Hotel Vintage Plaza features charming, European-style elegance. Built in 1894, this hotel is listed on the historical registry and offers a dramatic atrium lobby and comfortable piano lounge.

Each guest room is stylishly appointed in rich color schemes with custom cherry furniture. There are nine unique two-story townhouse suites, boasting solarium-style windows to capture the spectacular views.

The Pazzo Ristorante offers a casually elegant setting, serving breakfast and lunch, as well as featuring innovative Northern Italian cuisine with an extensive wine list.

Marriott Downtown

Marriott Downtown
1401 Southwest Front Avenue
Portland, Oregon 97201
800-228-9290 • (503) 226-7600

Room Rates:	$119 – $175. AAA discount.
Pet Charges or Deposits:	None.
Rated: 4 Paws 🐾🐾🐾🐾	503 guest rooms and 6 suites on the waterfront, heated indoor swimming pool, health club with whirlpool, sauna and exercise room, restaurants and cocktail lounge.

C onveniently located only minutes from the heart of town on the banks of the Willamette River, this gracious hotel offers deluxe guest rooms with panoramic views of the river and city.

Diversions abound inside the hotel. Guests will enjoy the indoor pool and working out in the health club with its sauna and whirlpool. The Waterfront Park, located only steps from the hotel, offers the best of downtown's shops and restaurants.

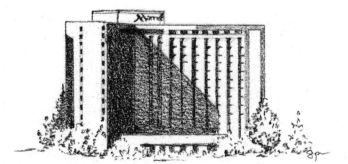

River Place Hotel

River Place Hotel
1510 Southwest Harbor Way
Portland, Oregon 97201
800-227-1333 • (503) 228-3233
Web Site: www.riverplacehotel.com

Room Rates:	$195 – $700, including continental breakfast. AAA discount.
Pet Charges or Deposits:	$100 per stay.
Rated: 5 Paws 🐾 🐾 🐾 🐾 🐾	39 deluxe rooms and 35 luxury suites, many with river views, 10 condominiums, 24-hour room service, athletic club, restaurant and bar.

T he waters of the Willamette River ripple past the River Place Hotel at the edge of downtown Portland. The rotunda roof and turrets overlook the adjacent marina and European-style, wood-frame neighborhood; green lawns slope down to meet the start of a two-mile waterfront park.

The warmth and attention to detail are apparent from the moment you enter the lobby with its hand-crafted rugs, grand floral arrangements and natural light. Choose from guest rooms, parlor suites or furnished condominiums. The Athletic Club offers racquetball courts, aerobic classes, a sauna and an indoor pool.

The Esplanade Restaurant, considered to be one of the city's finest, offers fine regional cuisine and extraordinary views of the river.

Ocean Locomotion on the Beach

Ocean Locomotion on the Beach
19130 Alder Avenue
Rockaway Beach, Oregon 97136
(503) 355-2093

Room Rates:	$37.50 – $170.
Pet Charges or Deposits:	$5 first day, $2 each additional day. Sorry, no cats.
Rated: 3 Paws 🐾 🐾 🐾	2 guest rooms and 8 cottages, ocean views, full kitchens, separate living rooms, fireplaces and decks.

L ocated near the oceanfront, with scenic views of Twin Rocks, each unit is unique, clean and comfortable. There are one-, two-, and three-bedroom cottages accommodating up to six people, with fully equipped kitchens and separate living areas, as well as two sleeper units with accommodations for two guests.

Be sure to venture down to the beach with your dog for some clamming. Rakes and buckets are available in the office. Feel free to use the barbecue or the firepit to have an old-fashioned clambake.

Phoenix Inn

Phoenix Inn
4370 Commercial Street
Salem, Oregon 97302
800-445-4498 • (503) 588-9220

Room Rates:	$65 – $105, including continental breakfast. AAA, AARP, AKC and ABA discounts.
Pet Charges or Deposits:	$10 per day.
Rated: 3 Paws 🐾 🐾 🐾	88 suites, indoor pool, Jacuzzi, fitness center, restaurant and lounge.

C onveniently located just south of downtown Salem, the Phoenix Inn offers guests spacious mini-suites complete with microwaves, refrigerators, wet bars, plush love seats and large worktables for those traveling on business.

The continental breakfast buffet is always complimentary at the Phoenix Inn. While reading your newspaper or watching the morning news, enjoy a selection of fruits, juices, coffee, cereals and pastries in the breakfast room.

Comfort Inn — Boardwalk

Comfort Inn — Boardwalk
545 Broadway
Seaside, Oregon 97138
800-228-5150 • (503) 738-3011

Room Rates:	$65 – $170, including continental breakfast and evening snacks. AAA, AARP, AKC and ABA discounts.
Pet Charges or Deposits:	None.
Rated: 3 Paws 🐾🐾🐾	57 guest rooms and 8 suites, most with balcony or patio overlooking the river, some with efficiency kitchens, gas fireplaces and whirlpools, laundry facilities, heated indoor swimming pool, sauna and whirlpool.

A long the banks of the Necanicum River and boardwalk, the Comfort Inn – Boardwalk offers guests comfortable, convenient, homey accommodations ranging from a roomy standard guest room to an efficiency or a whirlpool suite.

The Inn offers a deluxe breakfast bar to start your day off right and evening snacks to welcome you back after your busy day of business meetings or sightseeing.

Located in downtown Seaside, the oldest ocean resort in Oregon, the inn overlooks the river and boardwalk and is only 3 blocks from the Pacific Ocean. The beach offers a variety of activities from volleyball, fishing and swimming to beachcombing.

Ocean View Resort – Best Western

Ocean View Resort – Best Western
414 North Prom
Seaside, Oregon 97138
800-234-8439 • (503) 738-3334

Room Rates:	$69 – $265. AAA and AARP discounts.
Pet Charges or Deposits:	$15 per day. Small pets only. Manager's approval required.
Rated: 3 Paws 🐾 🐾 🐾	84 guest rooms and 20 suites, ocean or mountain views, some with gas fireplaces, kitchenettes, whirlpool tub, Jacuzzis, heated indoor pool and spa, restaurant and lounge.

T he tastefully decorated guest rooms offer spectacular views of either the Pacific Ocean or lush green mountains. Some rooms have the added amenities of a spacious living room, gas fireplace, oversized whirlpool tubs or kitchenette.

When it comes to recreation activities, you'll find plenty to do here. The hotel's heated indoor swimming pool and spa are inviting. Be sure to explore the shops and historical attractions that the charming town of Seaside has to offer.

DoubleTree Hotel – Eugene-Springfield

DoubleTree Hotel – Eugene-Springfield
3280 Gateway Road
Springfield, Oregon 97477
800-222-TREE • (541) 726-8181
Web Site: www.doubletreehotels.com

Room Rates:	$74 – $125. AAA and AARP discounts.
Pet Charges or Deposits:	None.
Rated: 3 Paws 🐾 🐾 🐾	227 guest rooms and 7 suites, heated pool, whirlpool, 2 tennis courts, restaurant and coffee shop.

K nown for its spacious, comfortable guest rooms and amenities that you would expect to find in a first-class hotel, the DoubleTree Hotel is a great choice for those visiting the Eugene-Springfield area. Comfortable accommodations will have either a balcony or a patio overlooking the attractively landscaped grounds.

Keep in shape while you are on vacation, at the hotel's health club. You can treat yourself to the on-site spa, play a few games of tennis, go for a swim in the heated pool, or relax by the pool and soak up some sun. Both you and your dog will enjoy the jogging and bicycling trails in the neighborhood parks. If you are visiting the area during ski season, the Willamette Pass Ski Area is easily accessible.

Rodeway Inn

Rodeway Inn
3480 Hutton Street
Springfield, Oregon 97477
800-363-8471 • (541) 746-8471

Room Rates:	$60 – $80, including continental breakfast. AAA and AARP discounts.
Pet Charges or Deposits:	$10 per stay. Call for deposit requirements.
Rated: 3 Paws 🐾 🐾 🐾	58 guest rooms, heated indoor pool and fitness facilities.

 Set in Springfield, near the Willamette River, the Rodeway Inn offers clean, comfortable and affordable rooms. A complimentary morning breakfast is included in your room rate. You will enjoy the inn's fitness facilities and heated indoor pool.

The location is convenient to historic towns, antique shops, fishing, golfing, white-water rafting, scenic bike trails and rural drives.

Quality Inn

Quality Inn
2114 West Sixth Street
P.O. Box 723
The Dalles, Oregon 97058
800-848-9378 • (541) 298-5161
Web Site: www.qualityinn.com

Room Rates:	$49 – $79. AAA and AARP discounts.
Pet Charges or Deposits:	$2 per day.
Rated: 3 Paws 🐾 🐾 🐾	85 guest rooms, many with kitchens, some fireplaces, heated swimming pool, whirlpool, health club privileges, restaurant and cocktail lounge.

 hether you're passing through on Interstate 84, or looking for a home base while exploring the beautiful Columbia River Gorge, the Quality Inn is a comfortable, reasonably priced place to stay.

Lying on a bend of the Columbia River, The Dalles offers many exciting things to do and see. The Dalles Lock and Dam features a guided tour of the area, including a train ride, and there is more than 9,000 acres for you and your dog to explore. So bring your boat and your water skis, pack a picnic lunch and make a day of it.

Wayfarer Resort

Wayfarer Resort
46725 Goodpasture Road
Vida, Oregon 97488
800-627-3613 • (541) 896-3613

Room Rates:	$75 – $195; packages available.
Pet Charges or Deposits:	$10. Small pets only.
Rated: 3 Paws 🐾 🐾 🐾	13 riverfront cottages with fully equipped kitchens and fireplaces, for up to 8 guests; large decks, laundry facilities and daily maid service available.

T he Wayfarer Resort offers a cozy home base for people who love to fish, hike, raft, boat, swim, play volleyball and tennis or simply commune with nature.

Located on the banks of the spectacular McKenzie River, the resort offers a choice of thirteen secluded, rustic cabins on ten private, wooded acres, with open-beamed ceilings, fully equipped kitchens and cozy fireplaces. Bask on spacious decks, the perfect place to sit back and enjoy the beauty of this natural setting and the solitude created among the snow-capped Cascades, surrounded by acres of forest.

Edgewater Cottages

Edgewater Cottages
3978 Southwest Pacific Coast Highway
Waldport, Oregon 97394
(541) 563-2240

Room Rates:	$65 – $140.
Pet Charges or Deposits:	$5 – $10 per pet, per day. Manager's approval required.
Rated: 4 Paws 🐾🐾🐾🐾	9 oceanfront or oceanview cottages and housekeeping units with kitchens, fireplaces and sun decks.

O n the sandy shores of Alsea Bay, Edgewater Cottages offers guests a change of pace from the usual vacation accommodations. These oceanfront cottages and housekeeping units have fully equipped kitchens, cozy fireplaces and wonderful sun decks.

Cottages range from intimate oceanview studios for two, to the Beachcomber, the largest unit, which offers three bedrooms, a living room with a large fireplace and a game room.

Shilo Inn

Shilo Inn
1609 East Harbor Drive
Warrenton, Oregon 97146
800-222-2244 • (503) 861-2181

Room Rates:	$85 – $149. AAA and AARP discounts.
Pet Charges or Deposits:	$7 per pet, per day.
Rated: 3 Paws 🐾🐾🐾	62 mini-suites, some efficiencies, heated swimming pool, sauna, steam room, whirlpool, exercise room, laundry facilities, restaurant and cocktail lounge.

W ith comfortable, convenient accommodations along Oregon's beautiful coastline, the Shilo Inn offers immaculate mini-suites at a moderate price.

The Inn's fitness center is available to guests so you won't miss your daily workout. Follow that with a relaxing soak in the spa or sauna, or an invigorating steam bath. The heated swimming pool is open 24 hours a day.

For your convenience, the Inn's Deli-Mart has a full range of items, just in case you have forgotten something, plus a variety of gifts, foods, specialty items, fishing licenses and tackle.

Old Welches Inn Bed and Breakfast

Old Welches Inn Bed and Breakfast
26401 East Welches Road
Welches, Oregon 97067
(503) 622-3754

Room Rates:	$75 – $175, including full breakfast.
Pet Charges or Deposits:	Credit card deposit. Manager's approval required. Sorry, no cats.
Rated: 4 Paws 🐾🐾🐾🐾	4 nonsmoking guest rooms, one with private bath; a private two-bedroom cottage with a fireplace and fully equipped kitchen, all with mountain or river views.

L ocated along the Salmon River in the Welches Valley, the heart of the Mount Hood Recreational Area, is the Old Welches Inn Bed and Breakfast. Built in 1890, the Inn was the first hotel and summer resort established on Mount Hood.

Choose from four guest rooms, all named after various wildflowers found in Oregon. Accommodations feature sleigh beds with fluffy comforters, heirloom furniture and views of the Salmon River. For those who want more privacy, the Lilybank Cottage is located behind the Inn. This private, two-bedroom cottage, residing under a 500-year-old Douglas fir tree, has a fully equipped kitchen, a river-rock fireplace and a fenced yard for the dog.

Holiday Inn Express

Holiday Inn Express
2887 Newburg Highway
Woodburn, Oregon 97071
800-766-6433 • (503) 982-6515
Web Site: www.holidayinnxpress.com/woodburn
E-mail: info@holidayinnxpress.com

Room Rates:	$65 – $85, including expanded continental breakfast. AAA, AARP, AKC and ABA discounts.
Pet Charges or Deposits:	$10 per day, up to $30.
Rated: 3 Paws 🐾🐾🐾	75 guest rooms and 6 suites with refrigerators and microwaves; heated pool, whirlpool and laundry facilities.

I n the heart of Oregon's wine country, the Holiday Inn Express offers comfortable rooms and spacious suites. An expanded, complimentary continental breakfast, featuring fresh-brewed coffee, hot tea, cold cereals, fresh fruit and pastries is served every morning.

You will want to explore the historical grandeur of the capital city of **Salem** and the breathtaking beauty of the Columbia River, located only a short drive from the Inn.

Flying M Ranch

Flying M Ranch
23029 Northwest Flying M Road
Yamhill, Oregon 97148
(503) 662-3222

Room Rates:	$70 – $200.
Pet Charges or Deposits:	Call for deposit requirements.
Rated: 3 Paws 🐾 🐾 🐾	28-room bunkhouse and 7 private cabins, some full kitchens, restaurant and cocktail lounge.

S tep back in time at this year-round resort, which embodies the spirit of the Oregon frontier. From the massive Douglas fir log lodges and cozy cabins, to the mouth-watering barbecue dinners along the trail, you can sample the life of our earliest settlers along the banks of the North Yamhill River. The ranch is set among the tall pine, alder and dogwood trees on 800 spectacular acres, where you and your dog can roam to your heart's content.

The ranch is located on part of the historic stagecoach trail that was once used for trips between Yamhill and Tillamook. Enjoy guided horseback rides for everyone from novice to advanced riders, great trout fishing, a large swimming pond and horseshoes. If you aren't too saddle sore, the Sawtooth Room features live country music and dance lessons to go with your favorite spirits.

Oregon

Please note: *Pets must be on a leash at all times and may be restricted to certain areas. For directions, use fees, pet charges and general information, contact the numbers listed below.*

National Parks General Information

Tourism Division
Oregon Department of Economic Development
775 Summer Street, Northeast
Salem, Oregon 97310
800-547-7842

Oregon Department of Fish and Wildlife
2501 Southwest First Street
P.O. Box 59
Portland, Oregon 97207
(503) 229-5403

National Parks

MEDFORD

Crater Lake National Park, located 72 miles east of Medford off Interstate 5 to State Route 62, is 183,224 acres of parkland offering picnic areas, fishing, hiking and bicycle trails, winter sports and a visitor's center. For more information, call (541) 5945-2211.

National Recreation Areas

JOSEPH

Hells Canyon National Recreation Area, located near Joseph, is 652,977 acres of parkland offering picnic areas, a boat ramp, fishing, swimming, hiking trails, winter sports and a visitor's center. For more information, call (541) 523-3356 or 800-523-1235. For road conditions, call (541) 426-4978.

BEND

Oregon Dunes National Recreation Area, located between North Bend and Florence, is a 32,000-acre park located within the Siuslaw National Forest. You will find picnic areas, a boat ramp, fishing, swimming, hiking trails and a visitor's center. For more information, call (541) 271-3611.

National Forest General Information

Bureau of Land Management
P.O. Box 2965
Portland, Oregon 97208
(503) 280-7001

Pacific Northwest Region
333 Southwest First Avenue
P.O. Box 3623
Portland, Oregon 97208
(503) 326-2877 – information
800-280-2267 – reservations

National Forests

BAKER CITY
Wallowa-Whitman National Forest encompasses 2,392,160 acres in northeastern Oregon and offers picnic areas, a boat ramp, boat rentals, fishing, swimming, horseback riding, hiking trails and winter sports. For more information, call (541) 523-6391.

BEND
Deschutes National Forest, located 6 miles south of Bend via U.S. Highway 97, has 1,602,609 acres of parkland offering picnic areas, a boat ramp, boat rentals, fishing, swimming, hiking and bicycle trails, horse rentals for pack and saddle trips, winter sports and a visitor's center. For more information, call (541) 388-2715.

CORVALLIS
Siulaw National Forest, located in western Oregon between Tillamook and Coos Bay, is a 630,000-acre parkland offering picnic areas, a boat ramp, fishing, swimming, hiking and bicycle trails, winter sports and a visitor's center. For more information, call (541) 750-7000.

EUGENE
Willamette National Forest encompasses 1,675,407 acres of parkland in western Oregon. Enjoy picnic areas, a boat ramp, boat rentals, fishing, swimming,

hiking and bicycle trails, winter sports and a visitor's center. For more information, call (541) 465-6521.

GRANTS PASS

Siskiyou National Forest encompasses 1,092,302 acres of parkland offering picnic areas, a boat ramp, fishing, swimming, hiking and bicycle trails, winter sports and a visitor's center. To gain access to the park from the west, take U.S. Highway 101; from the north and south take Interstate 5. For more information, call (541) 471-6500.

JOHN DAY

Malheur National Forest, located in eastern Oregon, offers 1,465,397 acres of parkland with picnic areas, a boat ramp, fishing, swimming, hiking trails, bicycle trails and winter sports. For more information, call (541) 575-3000.

KLAMATH FALLS

Winema National Forest, located in south-central Oregon off U.S. Highway 97 North or State Route Highway 140 West, encompasses 1,039,093 acres of parkland offering picnic areas, a boat ramp, boat rentals, fishing, swimming, hiking and bicycle trails, winter sports and a visitor's center. For more information, call (541) 883-6714.

LAKEVIEW

Fremont National Forest, located in south-central Oregon, has 1,200,679 acres of parkland with picnic areas, a boat ramp, fishing, swimming, hiking trails, bicycle trails and winter sports. For more information, call (541) 947-2151 or 947-6359.

MEDFORD

Rogue River National Forest, located off Interstate 5, is a 629,088-acre park offering picnic areas, a boat ramp, boat rentals, fishing, swimming, hiking trails, bicycle trails and winter sports. For more information, call (541) 858-2200.

PENDLETON

Umatilla National Forest, extending from northeast to southeastern Oregon, encompasses 1,402,483 acres of parkland offering picnic areas, a boat ramp, fishing, swimming, hiking and bicycle trails, horse rentals, winter sports and a visitor's center. For more information, call (541) 278-3716.

PORTLAND

Mount Hood National Forest may be entered from State Route 26 or Interstate 205 to State Route 212 and State Route 224. The Hood River entrance to the forest is off State Route 35 South. Mount Hood is 1.1 million acres of parkland in northwestern Oregon offering alpine skiing, camping, hiking and river running. For more information, call (503) 666-0771.

PRINEVILLE

Ochoco National Forest, located in central Oregon, is a 959,317-acre park offering picnic areas, a boat ramp, boat rentals, fishing, swimming, hiking and bicycle trails, winter sports and a visitor's center. From Prineville, take U.S. Highway 26, which cuts through Grassland to Madras, to gain access to the forest. For more information, call (541) 461-6500.

ROSEBURG

Umpqua National Forest, located 33 miles east of Roseburg on State Route 138, is a 984,602-acre park offering picnic areas, a boat ramp, boat rentals, fishing, swimming, hiking and bicycle trails, winter sports and a visitor's center. For more information, call (541) 672-6601.

Army Corps of Engineers

BLUE RIVER

Blue River Lake, located off State Route 126, is a 1,420-acre park offering picnic areas, a boat ramp, fishing, swimming and water-skiing.

Cougar Lake, located southeast of Blue River off State Route 126 and West Side Road, is a 1,280-acre park offering picnic areas, a boat ramp, fishing, swimming and hiking trails.

COTTAGE GROVE

Cottage Grove Reservoir, located 6 miles south of Cottage Grove via Interstate 5, offers picnic areas, a boat ramp, water-skiing, fishing and swimming. For more information, call (541) 942-2411.

Dorena Reservoir, located 5 miles east of Cottage Grove off Interstate 5, offers picnic areas, a boat ramp, boat rentals, fishing and swimming.

DETROIT

Detroit Lake, located off State Route 22, encompasses 3,500 acres of parkland with picnic areas, a boat ramp, water-skiing, fishing, swimming and hiking trails.

DEXTER

Dexter Lake, located off State Route 58, offers picnic areas, a boat ramp, boat rentals, water-skiing, fishing and swimming.

Lookout Point Lake, located south of Dexter off State Route 58, encompasses 4,360 acres with picnic areas, a boat ramp, fishing and swimming.

EUGENE

Fern Ridge Reservoir, located 12 miles east of Eugene off State Route 126, encompasses 9,000 acres of parkland with picnic areas, a boat ramp, boat rentals, fishing, swimming and water-skiing. For more information, call the Convention and Visitors Association of Lake County, Oregon, at (541) 484-5307 or 800-547-5445.

MEDFORD

Applegate Lake, located 23 miles southwest of Medford via State Route 238, is a 205-acre park offering picnic areas, a boat ramp, fishing, swimming and hiking trails.

Lost Creek Lake, located 30 miles northeast of Medford, via State Route 62, has 3,430 acres of parkland with picnic areas, a boat ramp, boat rentals, water-skiing, fishing, swimming, hiking trails and a visitor's center.

OAKRIDGE

Hills Creek Lake, southeast of Oakridge off State Route 58 and Rigdon Road, encompasses 2,710 acres and offers picnic areas, a boat ramp, water-skiing, fishing and swimming.

PORTLAND

Bonnieville Lock and Dam, located 40 miles east of Portland via Interstate 84, Exit 40, encompasses 206,000 acres of parkland with picnic areas, a boat ramp, boat rentals, fishing, hiking trails and a visitor's center. For more information, call (541) 374-8820.

RUFUS

John Day Lock and Dam, located 2 miles east of Rufus off Interstate 84, Exit 109, offers 31,041 acres with picnic areas, a boat ramp, boat rentals, water-skiing, fishing and swimming. For more information, call (541) 296-1181.

SPRINGFIELD

Fall Creek Lake, located 16 miles southeast of Springfield via Jasper Lowell Road, encompasses 1,820 acres of parkland offering picnic areas, a boat ramp, fishing, swimming and water-skiing. For more information, call the Convention and Visitors Association of Lake County, Oregon, at 800-547-5445 or (541) 484-5307.

SWEET HOME

Foster Lake, located off U.S. Highway 20 at Sweet Home, encompasses 1,220 acres of parkland offering picnic areas, a boat ramp, water-skiing, fishing, swimming, winter sports and a visitor's center.

Green Peter Lake, northeast of Sweet Home off Quartzville Road, encompasses 3,720 acres of parkland with picnic areas, a boat ramp, boat rentals, fishing, swimming and water-skiing.

THE DALLES

The Dalles Lock and Dam, located off Interstate 84, Exit 87, on the edge of The Dalles, offers picnic areas, a boat ramp, boat rentals, water-skiing, fishing, swimming and a visitor's center. For more information, call 800-255-3385 or (541) 296-2231.

UMATILLA

McNary Lock and Dam, located 1 mile east of junction Interstate 82 and U.S. Highway 730, encompasses 9,718 acres of parkland with picnic areas, a boat ramp, water-skiing, fishing and swimming. For more information, call (541) 922-4388.

State Parks General Information

Oregon Department of Parks and Recreation
1115 Commercial Street, Northeast
Salem, Oregon 97310
800-551-6949 – information
800-452-5687 – reservations

State Parks

BAKER CITY

Sumpter Valley Dredge State Park is an 83-acre park located 29 miles southwest of Baker City on State Route 7. The park offers areas for picnicking, hiking and winter sports.

BANDON

Bullards Beach State Park, located 1 mile north of Bandon on U.S. Highway 101, encompasses 1,226 acres of parkland with picnic areas, a boat ramp, fishing, swimming, hiking and bicycle trails. For more information, call (541) 347-9616.

BEND

Tumalo State Park is a 320-acre park within the Deschutes National Forest, located 5.5 miles north of Bend, off U.S. Highway 20. The park offers picnic areas, fishing, swimming and hiking trails. For more information, call (541) 388-2715 or 800-388-5664.

BROOKINGS

Harris Beach State Park is a 171-acre park located 2 miles north of Brookings on U.S. Highway 101. The park offers picnic areas, fishing, swimming and hiking trails.

Loeb State Park, located 8 miles northeast of Brookings off U.S. Highway 101, is a 320-acre park offering picnic areas, fishing, swimming and hiking trails.

Samuel H. Boardman State Park, located 6 miles north of Brookings on U.S. Highway 101, encompasses 1,473 acres of parkland with picnic areas, fishing and hiking trails.

CANNON BEACH

Ecola State Park encompasses 1,303 acres of parkland, located 2 miles north of Cannon Beach off U.S. Highway 101. The park offers picnic areas, fishing and hiking trails. For more information, call (503) 436-2844.

CHARLESTON

Cape Arago State Park, located 5 miles south of Charleston, is a 134-acre park with picnic areas, fishing and hiking trails.

CHILOQUIN

Collier Memorial State Park, located near Chiloquin on U.S. Highway 97, consists of 655 acres of parkland with picnic areas, fishing, hiking trails and a visitor's center. For more information, call (541) 783-2471.

COOS BAY

Golden and Silver Falls State Park is a 157-acre park in the Coast Range, located 24 miles northeast of Coos Bay, off U.S. Highway 101. Visitors to the park will find two waterfalls, an old-growth forest, picnic areas, fishing and hiking trails. For more information, call (541) 888-3778 or 800-824-8486.

William H. Tugman State Park, located 19 miles north of Coos Bay on U.S. Highway 101, is a 560-acre park offering picnic areas, a boat ramp, boat rentals, fishing and swimming.

DEPOE BAY

Fogarty Creek is a 142-acre park located 2 miles north of Depoe Bay along U.S. Highway 101. Visitors to the park will find picnic areas, fishing and hiking trails. For more information, call (503) 436-2844.

DETROIT

Detroit Lake State Park is a 104-acre park located 2 miles west of Detroit on State Route 22, offering picnic areas, a boat ramp, boat rentals, fishing and swimming.

ELGIN

Minam State Park is a 602-acre park located 15 miles northeast of Elgin, off State Route 82. The park offers areas for picnicking and fishing.

ESTACADA

Milo McIver State Park encompasses 937 acres of parkland, located 5 miles west of Estacada, off State Route 211. Visitors to the park will enjoy picnic areas, a boat ramp, fishing and hiking trails.

EUGENE

Armitage State Park, located 5 miles north of Eugene on Coburg Road, is a 57-acre park offering picnic areas, a boat ramp, fishing and hiking.

Ben and Kay Dorris State Park, located 31 miles east of Eugene on State Route 126, consists of 92 acres of parkland with picnic areas, boating, fishing and hiking trails.

Elijah Bristow State Park encompasses 848 acres and is located 15 miles southeast of Eugene on State Route 58. It has picnic areas, fishing and hiking trails.

Hendricks Bridge State Park is a 17-acre park located 13 miles east of Eugene on State Route 126. The park offers picnic areas, a boat ramp and fishing.

FLORENCE

Carl G. Washburne Memorial State Park, located 14 miles north of Florence on U.S. Highway 101, is a 1,089-acre park offering picnic areas, fishing, swimming and hiking trails.

Devil's Elbow State Park is a 545-acre park located 13 miles north of Florence on U.S. Highway 101. The park offers picnic areas, fishing and hiking trails.

Jessie M. Honeyman Memorial State Park is a 522-acre park located 2.5 miles south of Florence off U.S. Highway 101. Visitors to the park will find picnic areas, a boat ramp, boat rentals, fishing, swimming and hiking trails.

LA GRANDE

Hilgard Junction State Park, located 8 miles west of La Grande off Interstate 84, encompasses 233 acres of parkland and offers areas for picnicking and fishing.

LAKE OSWEGO

Mary S. Young State Park is a 133-acre park located 3 miles south of Lake Oswego on State Route 43. Enjoy picnic areas, fishing and hiking and bicycle trails.

HAMMOND

Fort Stevens State Park encompasses 3,763 acres of parkland, located 10 miles west of Hammond on U.S. Highway 101 near Warrenton. You will find picnic areas, a boat ramp, fishing, clamming, swimming, hiking and bicycle trails and a visitor's center.

HUNTINGTON

Farewell Bend State Park is a 72-acre park located 4 miles south of Huntington, off Interstate 84. The park offers picnic areas, a boat ramp, fishing and swimming.

JOHN DAY

Clyde Holliday State Park is a 15-acre park located 7 miles west of John Day on U.S. Highway 26. Enjoy the area for picnics and fishing.

JOSEPH

Wallowa Lake State Park, located 6 miles south of Joseph on State Route 82, encompasses 166 acres of parkland with picnic areas, a boat ramp, boat rentals, fishing, swimming and hiking and bicycle trails.

KLAMATH FALLS

Jackson F. Kimball State Park is a 19-acre park located 3 miles north of Klamath Falls off State Route 232. You will find picnic areas, fishing and hiking trails.

LA PINE

La Pine State Park, located 8.5 miles north of La Pine and 27 miles south of Bend, encompasses 2,008 acres of parkland within the borders of the Deschutes National Forest. Visitors to the park will find picnic areas, a boat ramp and fishing. For more information, call (541) 388-2715 or 388-5664.

LAKEVIEW

Goose Lake State Park is a 64-acre park located 15 miles southwest of Lakeview, off U.S. Highway 395. The park offers picnic areas, a boat ramp and fishing.

LINCOLN CITY

Devil's Lake State Park, located at Lincoln City on U.S. Highway 101, is a 109-acre park offering picnic areas, a boat ramp, fishing and swimming.

MADRAS

The Cove Palisades State Park encompasses 4,130 acres of parkland located 15 miles southwest of Madras off U.S. Highway 97. The park offers picnic areas, a boat ramp, boat rentals, fishing, swimming, hiking trails and winter sports. For more information, call (541) 546-3412.

MANZANITA

Nehalem Bay State Park, located 3 miles south of Manzanita off U.S. Highway 101, offers 878 acres of parkland with picnic areas, a boat ramp, fishing, swimming and bicycle trails.

Oswald West State Park encompasses 2,474 acres of parkland, located 5 miles north of Manzanita on U.S. Highway 101. This historic area offers picnic areas, fishing, clamming, swimming and hiking trails.

MEACHAM

Emigrant Springs State Park is a 23-acre park located 3 miles northwest of Meacham on Interstate 84. Enjoy picnic areas, hiking trails and a visitor's center.

MEDFORD

Casey State Park, an 80-acre park located 29 miles northeast of Medford on State Route 62, offers picnic areas, a boat ramp, fishing and swimming.

Joseph P. Stewart State Park, located 35 miles northeast of Medford off State Route 62, offers picnic areas, a boat ramp, boat rentals, fishing, swimming and hiking and bicycle trails.

Prospect Wayside State Park is a 6-acre park located 44 miles east of Medford off State Route 62. It offers areas for picnicking, fishing and hiking trails.
Tou Velle State Park, located 9 miles north of Medford off State Route 62, is a 51-acre park offering picnic areas, a boat ramp and fishing.

MILL CITY

North Santiam State Park is a 120-acre park located 4 miles west of Mill City off State Route 22. The park offers picnic areas, fishing and hiking trails.

NECANICUM

Saddle Mountain State Park, located 8 miles northeast of Necanicum off U.S. Highway 26, consists of 2,882 acres of parkland. The park offers panoramic views of the Coast Range, areas for picnicking and trails for hiking.

NEWBERG

Champoeg State Park encompasses 587 acres of parkland on the Willamette River, 7 miles east of Newberg, off U.S. Highway 99 West. Visitors to the park will find picnic areas, boating, fishing, a visitor's center and hiking and bicycle trails. For more information, call (503) 678-1251 or 678-1649.

NEWPORT

Beverly Beach State Park, located 7 miles north of Newport on U.S. Highway 101, encompasses 130 acres of parkland with picnic areas, fishing and hiking trails.

Ona Beach State Park is a 237-acre park located 8 miles south of Newport on U.S. Highway 101. Visitors to the park will find picnic areas, a boat ramp and fishing.

Seal Rock Wayside State Park, located 10 miles south of Newport on U.S. Highway 101, consists of 7 acres of parkland with areas for picnicking, fishing and hiking.

South Beach State Park is a 411-acre park located 2 miles south of Newport on U.S. Highway 101. The park offers areas for picnicking, fishing and hiking.

NORTH BEND

Sunset Bay State Park, located 2 miles southwest of North Bend, is a 395-acre park offering picnic areas, fishing, swimming and hiking trails.

NYSSA

Lake Owyhee State Park is a 730-acre park located 33 miles southwest of Nyssa off State Route 301. Enjoy the picnic areas, a boat ramp, boat rentals and fishing.

Creek State Park, located 30 miles south of Nyssa off State Route 201, encompasses 1,910 acres of parkland with picnic areas and hiking trails.

ONTARIO

Ontario State Park is located 1 mile north of Ontario on Interstate 84. The park consists of 35 acres and offers picnic areas, boating and fishing.

PACIFIC CITY

Cape Kiwanda State Park, located 1 mile north of Pacific City, off U.S. Highway 101, is a scenic park consisting of 185 acres. Visitors will find boating, fishing and hiking trails.

PORT ORFORD

Cape Blanco State Park, located 9 miles north of Port Orford, then 6 miles west off U.S. Highway 101, is an 1,880-acre park offering picnic areas, fishing and hiking trails.

Humbug Mountain State Park encompasses 1,842 acres of parkland overlooking the Pacific Ocean, located 6 miles south of Port Orford on U.S. Highway 101. You will find picnic areas, scuba diving, whale-watching, fishing, swimming and hiking trails. For more information, call (503) 332-6774.

PORTLAND

Ainsworth State Park, located 37 miles east of Portland on U.S. Highway 30, has 156 acres of scenic parkland with picnic areas and hiking trails.

Benson State Park, located 30 miles east of Portland off Interstate 84, is a 272-acre park offering picnic areas, a boat ramp, fishing and swimming.

Dabney State Park is a 135-acre park located 19 miles east of Portland on U.S. Highway 30. The park offers picnic areas, a boat ramp, fishing and hiking trails. Lewis and Clark State Park is a 56-acre park located 16 miles east of Portland off Interstate 84. The park offers picnic areas, a boat ramp, fishing, hiking trails and a visitor's center.

Rooster Rock State Park, located 22 miles east of Portland off Interstate 84, encompasses 927 acres of parkland with picnic areas, a boat ramp, fishing, swimming and hiking trails.

Tryon Creek State Park is located 6 miles southwest of Portland off Interstate 5 on Terwilliger Boulevard. This 627-acre park offers hiking and bicycle trails, winter sports and a visitor's center.

PRINEVILLE

Ochoco Lake State Park is a 10-acre park located 7 miles east of Prineville on U.S. Highway 26. The park offers picnic areas, a boat ramp, fishing and hiking trails, plus winter sports such as cross-country skiing and snowmobiling.

Reservoir State Park encompasses 365 acres of parkland, located 17 miles southeast of Prineville off U.S. Highway 26. Enjoy picnic areas, a boat ramp, fishing, swimming, hiking trails and winter sports.

REDMOND

Smith Rock State Park is located 9 miles northeast of Redmond on U.S. Highway 97 to Terrebonne, then 3 miles east and follow the signs. This 623-acre park offers scenic views of colorful cliffs above the Crooked River, picnic areas, rock climbing, fishing and hiking.

REEDSPORT

Umpqua Lighthouse State Park, located 6 miles south of Reedsport off U.S. Highway 101, consists of 450 acres of parkland with visitors 2.5 miles of shoreline. It has sand dunes reaching up to 500 feet, plus picnic areas, boating, fishing, swimming and hiking trails.

Umpqua Wayside State Park is a 95-acre park located 7 miles east of Reedsport on State Route 38. The park offers areas for picnicking, a boat ramp and fishing.

ROGUE RIVER

Valley of the Rogue State Park is a 275-acre park located 3 miles south of Rogue River off Interstate 5. The park consists of areas for picnicking, a boat ramp and fishing.

SALEM

Silver Falls State Park, located 26 miles east of Salem on State Route 214, consists of 8,546 acres of parkland with picnic areas, fishing, swimming, hiking and bicycle trails, plus a visitor's center.

Willamette Mission State Park consists of 1,686 acres of parkland, located 8 miles north of Salem on Wheatland Ferry Road. You will find picnic areas, a boat ramp, fishing, hiking and bicycle trails.

SWEET HOME

Cascadia State Park, located 14 miles east of Sweet Home on U.S. Highway 20, consists of 253 acres of parkland offering picnic areas, fishing and hiking trails.

THE DALLES

Deschutes River State Park, located 17 miles east of The Dalles off Interstate 84, encompasses 515 acres of parkland with picnic areas, a boat ramp, fishing, white-water rafting and hiking trails.

Mayer State Park is a 613-acre park located 10 miles west of The Dalles off Interstate 84. Enjoy picnic areas, a boat ramp, fishing and swimming.

Shelton Wayside State Park, located 10 miles southeast of The Dalles off State Route 19, is a 180-acre park offering areas for picnicking and hiking.

TILLAMOOK

Cape Lookout State Park, located 12 miles southwest of Tillamook off U.S. Highway 101, encompasses 1,974 acres of parkland with picnic areas, fishing, clamming and hiking trails.

UMATILLA

Hat Rock State Park encompasses 735 acres of parkland, located 9 miles east of Umatilla off U.S. Highway 730. The park offers picnic areas, a boat ramp, fishing, swimming, hiking trails and winter sports.

UNION

Catherine Creek State Park is a 160-acre park located 8 miles southeast of Union on State Route 203. Visitors to the park will find areas for picnics and fishing.

UNITY JUNCTION

Unity Lake State Park is a 39-acre park located 5 miles north of Unity Junction on State Route 7. You will find areas for picnicking, a boat ramp and fishing.

WALDPORT

Beachside State Park, located 4 miles south of Waldport on U.S. Highway 101, is a 17-acre park offering picnic areas and fishing.

Governor Patterson Memorial State Park is a 10-acre park located 1 mile south of Waldport on U.S. Highway 101. The park offers picnic areas, fishing and hiking trails.

YACHATS

Neptune State Park, located 3 miles south of Yachats on U.S. Highway 101, is a 302-acre park offering picnic areas, fishing, swimming and hiking trails.

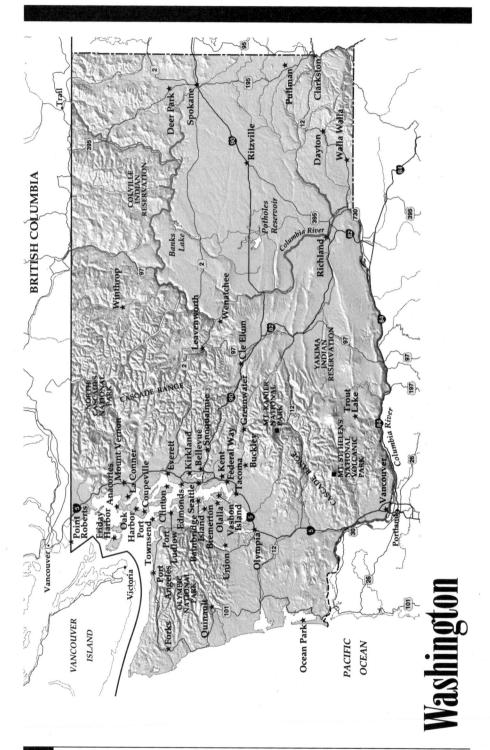

Washington

Pacific Northwest – Washington

Anacortes –
Fidalgo Country Inn...87
Old Brook Inn...88

Bainbridge Island –
Island Country Inn...89

Bremerton –
Quality Inn...90

Buckley –
Mount View Inn...91

Clarkston –
Highland House...92

Cle Elum –
Stewart Lodge...93

Clinton –
Home by the Sea Cottages...94

Coupeville –
Victorian Bed and Breakfast...95

Dayton –
Purple House Bed and Breakfast...96
Weinhard Hotel...97

Deer Park –
Love's Victorian Bed and Breakfast...98

Edmonds –
Edmonds Harbor Inn...99

Federal Way –
Federal Way Executel – Best Western...100

Fir Island –
South Fork Moorage – Guest
Houseboats...101

Forks –
Kalaloch Lodge...102

Friday Harbor –
Inn at Friday Harbor...103
Tucker House Bed and Breakfast with
Cottages...104
West Winds Harmony Cottage...105
Wharfside Bed and Breakfast Aboard the
"Jacquelyn"...106

Greenwater –
Alta Crystal Resort...107

Kent –
Howard Johnson Inn...108

Kirkland –
La Quinta Inn...109

La Conner –
Country Inn...110

Leavenworth –
Der Ritterhof Motor Inn...111

Mount Vernon –
College Way Inn – Best Western...112
CottonTree Inn – Best Western...113

Oak Harbor –
Harbor Pointe Bed and Breakfast...114

Ocean Park –
Sunset View Resort...115

Olalla –
Olalla Orchard Bed and Breakfast...116

Olympia –
Cinnamon Rabbit Bed and Breakfast...117

Puget View Guesthouse...118

Point Roberts –
Cedar House Inn Bed and Breakfast...119

Port Angeles –
DoubleTree Hotel...120
Log Cabin Resort...121
Maple Rose Inn...122

Port Ludlow –
Inn at Ludlow Bay...123

Port Townsend –
Palace Hotel...124
Swan Hotel and Conference Center...125

Pullman –
Heritage Inn – Best Western...126
Holiday Inn Express...127

Quinault –
Lake Quinault Lodge...128

Richland –
Hanford House – DoubleTree Hotel...129

Ritzville –
Heritage Inn – Best Western...130

Seattle –
Alexis Hotel...131
Four Seasons Olympic Hotel...132
Residence Inn by Marriott – Fairview Avenue
   North...133

Snoqualmie –
Salish Lodge and Spa...134

Spokane –
A Spokane Bed and Breakfast Service...135
Cavanaugh's River Inn...136
Thunderbird Inn – Best Western...137

Tacoma/Fife –
Royal Coachman Inn...138
Shilo Inn...139

Trout Lake –
Llama Ranch Bed and Breakfast...140

Union –
Alderbrook Resort...141

Vancouver –
Shilo Inn – Downtown...142
Shilo Inn – Hazel Dell...143

Vashon Island –
Swallow's Nest Guest Cottages...144

Walla Walla –
Comfort Inn...145

Wenatchee –
Heritage Inn – Best Western...146

Winthrop –
Cascade Inn – Best Western...147

Fidalgo Country Inn

Fidalgo Country Inn
1250 Highway 20
Anacortes, Washington 98221
(360) 293-3494
Web Site: www.NWCountryInns.com/Fidalgo
E-mail: nwcinns@seanet.com

Room Rates:	$69 – $189, including continental breakfast. AAA, AARP, AKC and ABA discounts.
Pet Charges or Deposits:	$10 – $20 per day.
Rated: 3 Paws 🐾🐾🐾	50 guest rooms and suites, some with refrigerators and microwaves, pool and Jacuzzi.

L ess than two hour's drive from Seattle or Vancouver, British Columbia, you will find the first of the San Juan Islands – Fidalgo Island. Anacortes acts as the hub of activities in the San Juan Islands and the inland areas of Skagit Valley. Fidalgo Country Inn is a good choice for those who want to enjoy it all.

The Inn is located just minutes from the Anacortes ferry terminal and Deception Pass on Whidbey Island. You will enjoy great golf here, plus boating, kayaking, parks, hiking, shopping and good restaurants.

All guest rooms and suites feature queen-or king-sized beds and a complimentary continental breakfast, and some have water views.

Old Brook Inn

Old Brook Inn
530 Old Brook Lane
Anacortes, Washington 98221
800-503-4768 • (360) 293-4768

Room Rates:	$80 – $90, including continental breakfast.
Pet Charges or Deposits:	None.
Rated: 4 Paws 🐾🐾🐾🐾	2 guest rooms with private baths and beautiful views of the woods or the bay.

S heltered in a valley of woods and green meadows, only three miles outside Anacortes, this enchanting inn is nestled within an heirloom orchard planted in 1868. The Inn takes its name form the small brook that meanders alongside it and winds throughout the tranquil ten acres.

Both guest rooms have scenic views of either the surrounding woods and orchards, or beautiful Fidalgo Bay. In the morning awake to a complimentary continental breakfast of fruit, hot muffins or coffee cake served in the dining room overlooking the orchard.

For the vigilant bird watcher, you will see hawks, eagles, osprey, kingfishers and great blue herons. The sightseeing doesn't end there. The San Juan Islands, only a short ferry ride away, are known as a vacation paradise.

Island Country Inn

Island Country Inn
920 Hildebrand Lane Northwest
Bainbridge Island, Washington 98110
(800) 842-8429 • 206-842-6861
Web Site: www.NWCountryInns.com/Island
E-mail: nwcinns@seanet.com

Room Rates:	$71 – $149, including continental breakfast. AAA, AARP, AKC and ABA discounts.
Pet Charges or Deposits:	$10 – $20 per day; credit card imprint required.
Rated: 3 Paws 🐾🐾🐾	40 guest rooms and 6 suites, kitchens, pool and Jacuzzi.

J ust 35 minutes by ferry from Seattle there's a quiet retreat — the Island Country Inn, the only hotel on Bainbridge Island. Guest rooms and suites feature queen- or king-sized beds, wet bars and kitchens. A complimentary continental breakfast is included in your room rate. Guests are encouraged to enjoy the heated outdoor pool in season, and the spa and patio area.

Historic Bainbridge Island is one of Puget Sound's most beautiful — tall timber, quiet farms, lovely homes and gardens, bays and harbors filled with pleasure boats. There's golf here, parks and playgrounds, a winery, shopping, art galleries, restaurants and hiking and biking trails to enjoy.

Quality Inn

Quality Inn
4303 Kitsap Way
Bremerton, Washington 98312-2025
800-776-2291 • (306) 405-1111

Room Rates:	$67 – $150, including continental breakfast. AAA and AARP discounts.
Pet Charges or Deposits:	$50 refundable deposit.
Rated: 3 Paws 🐾🐾🐾	103 guest rooms, some with efficiency or full kitchens, laundry facilities and whirlpools; heated swimming pool, Jacuzzi and fitness facilities.

S et in the heart of the Kitsap Peninsula on the western shore of Puget Sound is the Quality Inn. The tastefully appointed rooms are located on tiered grounds in five separate buildings, guaranteeing guests peace and quiet. Families will appreciate the apartment-sized units with kitchens and laundry facilities, as well as separate bedrooms.

Guests are welcome to take advantage of the fitness facilities, complete with bikes, rowing machines and weights, as well as the outdoor Jacuzzi and swimming pool. A complimentary continental breakfast is served in the lobby every morning, offering guests cereal, toast, muffins, fresh coffee and juice.

Mount View Inn

Mount View Inn
29405 Highway 410 East
P.O. Box J
Buckley, Washington 98321
800-582-4111 • (360) 829-1100

Room Rates:	$45 – $75, including continental breakfast. AAA, AARP, AKC and ABA discounts.
Pet Charges or Deposits:	$10 per stay.
Rated: 3 Paws 🐾🐾🐾	41 guest rooms and suites, some whirlpool tubs, laundry facilities, heated outdoor swimming pool and spa.

T he Mount View Inn provides comfortable luxury at an affordable price. Each of the guest rooms and suites has been tastefully designed and beautifully decorated with your comfort in mind. If you are looking for something special, the luxury suites offer a private whirlpool spa.

Buckley is the gateway to the Puget Sound area and spectacular Mount Rainier National Park, a striking landmark of the Pacific Northwest. For snow-skiing, nearby Crystal Mountain is a premier ski area. You will find no better place to go hiking than the Carbon River.

Highland House

Highland House
707 Highland Avenue
Clarkston, Washington 99403
(509) 758-3126

Room Rates:	$45 – $85, including full breakfast and high tea.
Pet Charges or Deposits:	$5 per stay, plus 10% of room rate as deposit. Cats must have carriers.
Rated: 3 Paws	5 guest rooms and 2 suites, large fenced yard, dog run, patio with barbecue, hot tub and common sitting room with fireplace.

A midst a delightful flower garden in a rural setting is the charming Colonial-style Highland House. Built in the 1890s, this inviting Victorian brings a bit of "Ye Olde England" to its guests.

The warm, friendly atmosphere extends to the guest rooms as well. Named after famous historical English counties, each of the well-appointed guest rooms offers that little extra touch of charm.

Guests are invited to spend time in the Yorkshire Room, where old pub games are played, or to sit by a comforting fire, the perfect place to relax with a good book. Located only minutes from the Inn are the Snake and Clearwater Rivers, a fisherman's paradise. For horseback riding, there are old Indian trails and prospectors' paths to explore, with various species of wildlife along the way.

Stewart Lodge

Stewart Lodge
805 West First Street
Cle Elum, Washington 98922
(509) 674-4548

Room Rates:	$45 – $60, including continental breakfast. AAA discount.
Pet Charges or Deposits:	$5 per stay.
Rated: 3 Paws	36 guest rooms, some refrigerators, laundry facilities, heated swimming pool, outdoor spa.

Filming site of the hit television series "Northern Exposure," the town of Cle Elum is home to the Stewart Lodge. This rustic-style inn features appealing guest rooms with a country decor, unique pine furnishings, quilted spreads and comfortable wingback chairs.

Known as the entrance to the Wenatchee and Mount Baker – Snoqualmie National Forests, the Cle Elum area offers recreation opportunities for everyone. You will find river raft and canoe trips down the 16-mile Yakima River, bicycling, river fishing, swimming, wind-surfing, lots of hiking trails to explore with your dog, horseback riding, rock hounding, snowmobiling and skiing.

Home by the Sea Cottages

Home by the Sea Cottages
2388 East Sunlight Beach Road
Clinton, Washington 98236
(360) 321-2964

Room Rates:	$165 – $175, including breakfast basket.
Pet Charges or Deposits:	None.
Rated: 5 Paws 🐾🐾🐾🐾🐾	A cottage with wood-burning fireplace, living room, small kitchen and full bath. Plus a private suite in the beachfront main house with kitchen, dining and living rooms, wood-burning stove, private deck and Jacuzzi.

L ocated on beautiful Whidbey Island, only steps from the beach, you will find the Home by the Sea Cottages. Guests may choose from two types of accommodations.

The Cape Cod Cottage is a 1940s-style beach cottage located just steps from Useless Bay. The main floor has a cozy cedar living room with a large wood-burning fireplace and views of Deer Lagoon. Upstairs there are two bedrooms, each with full-sized beds and views of the pasture and farmlands. The small country kitchen is great for relaxing with your morning cup of coffee and your complimentary breakfast basket, filled with homemade specialties using local products when in season.

The Sandpiper Suite is located in the main house on the beach. It has its own private garden entrance and a private outdoor Jacuzzi and deck that are perfect for those relaxing weekend getaways. With both properties so close to the beach, you and your dog can enjoy long walks on the driftwood-strewn beach.

Victorian Bed and Breakfast

Victorian Bed and Breakfast
P.O. Box 761
602 North Main Street
Coupeville, Washington 98239
(360) 678-5305

Room Rates: $85 – $100, including full breakfast.
Pet Charges or Deposits: Manager's approval required. Credit card as deposit.
Rated: 4 Paws   2 guest rooms with private baths and a secluded cottage with
         full kitchen and bath.

P lan to be pampered during your stay here. Enjoy a gourmet breakfast, relax in the courtyard and stroll historic Coupeville. Built in the late 1800s, the Victorian Bed and Breakfast is a charming Italianate Victorian home on Whidbey Island.

The Jenne and the Blue Goose Rooms, both with comfortable, queen-sized beds and private bathrooms, are located upstairs. For the ultimate in privacy, stay in the Cottage Hideaway, with a full kitchen and private bathroom. It has a queen-sized bed and a trundle bed, perfect for a child.

The heritage of the town of Coupeville is quite colorful. Known as the City of Sea Captains, due to the many seafaring settlers, the town blends its unique maritime history and vigorous pioneer spirit with its early Native American lore.

Purple House Bed and Breakfast

Purple House Bed and Breakfast
415 East Clay Street
Dayton, Washington 99328
800-486-2574 • (509) 382-3159

Room Rates:	$85 – $125, including full breakfast.
Pet Charges or Deposits:	Call for deposit requirements. Small dogs only. Sorry, no cats.
Rated: 3 Paws 🐾🐾🐾	4 guest rooms and 2 suites with shared or private baths, common rooms, beautifully landscaped grounds, dog run, heated outdoor swimming pool and patio.

T his elegant Queen Anne-style 1882 mansion blends the best of yesteryear with today's modern conveniences. Guests are welcome to relax in the library or in the spacious parlor, surrounded by art and period antiques.

With a hostess who loves to cook and draws upon her vast culinary repertoire, your morning feast will leave you well satisfied. For extended stays, she will pamper you with exquisitely prepared full-course dinners as well.

The Dayton area lends itself perfectly to the outdoor life, with plenty of fishing, hiking and winter skiing.

Weinhard Hotel

Weinhard Hotel
235 East Main Street
Dayton, Washington 99328
(509) 382-4032

Room Rates:	$65 – $125, including continental breakfast. AAA discount.
Pet Charges or Deposits:	None.
Rated: 4 Paws 🐾🐾🐾🐾	15 guest rooms, rooftop garden, lobby Espresso Café; non-smoking hotel.

As you enter through the brick archway of the Weinhard Hotel, with its antique coach lights and ornate, massive oak door, you are taken back in time to the late 19th century, when this beautiful old building was the town saloon and lodge hall. Now this elegant Victorian, nestled in the heart of historic Dayton, is a blending of modern comfort and elegance.

The unique guest rooms feature an exquisite collection of Victorian-American furniture with all the modern conveniences you expect to find in a fine hotel. Guests are invited to enjoy the gracious splendor of the Victorian roof garden with its potted flowers and comfortable, Adirondack-style chairs, while tasting a flavorful latté from the Weinhard Espresso Café.

Love's Victorian Bed and Breakfast

Love's Victorian Bed and Breakfast
31317 North Cedar Road
Deer Park, Washington 99006
888-929-2999 • (509) 276-6939

Room Rates: $75 – $98, including full breakfast.
Pet Charges or Deposits: Call for deposit requirements.
Rated: 4 Paws 🐾 🐾 🐾 🐾   2 guest rooms with private baths.

Set on five wooded acres overlooking a pond, this gracious, gabled Victorian resides, complete with gingerbread trim and a wraparound porch. When you cross the threshold, you will be transformed back in time. Love's Victorian Bed and Breakfast is an ornate home that reflects the turn-of-the-century style.

The two guest rooms are the Turret Suite, with a gas fireplace, a sitting area, private bath and a balcony overlooking the pond, and Annie's Room, named after Leslie's grandmother, with period wallpaper, lace curtains and a private bath.

The main-floor hot tub beckons visitors to relax and enjoy a view of the moon and stars through the overhead transom window.

Edmonds Harbor Inn

Edmonds Harbor Inn
130 West Dayton Street
Edmonds, Washington 98020
800-441-8033 • (425) 771-5021
Web Site: www.NWCountryInns.com/Harbor
E-mail: nwcinns@seanet.com

Room Rates:	$71 – $149, including continental breakfast. AAA, AARP, AKC and ABA discounts.
Pet Charges or Deposits:	$10 – $20 per day.
Rated: 3 Paws 🐾🐾🐾	60 guest rooms and suites with refrigerators and microwaves; health club privileges, including indoor pool and spa.

L ocated midway between Seattle and Everett, Edmonds is just 25 minutes to either. The Harbor Inn is located 11/2 blocks from the waterfront in the heart of Edmonds, with all its attractions and activities.

Perhaps one of the most picturesque small towns in Washington, Edmonds offers breathtaking views of the Olympic Mountains and snow-capped Mount Baker. Here you can walk your dog on beautiful beaches, watch ferry boats crossing Puget Sound and fish for salmon from the public pier and marina. Edmonds is noted for unique specialty shops and art galleries, antiques and many fine waterfront restaurants.

Each of the deluxe guest rooms and suites, some with kitchenettes, are comfortable and competitively priced. A complimentary continental breakfast is included in your room rate.

Federal Way Executel – Best Western

Federal Way Executel – Best Western
31611 20th Avenue South
Federal Way, Washington 98003
800-346-2874 • (253) 941-6000

Room Rates:	$89 – $149. AAA, AARP, AKC and ABA discounts.
Pet Charges or Deposits:	$20 per stay.
Rated: 3 Paws 🐾🐾🐾	112 guest rooms and 2 suites, heated outdoor swimming pool and hot tub, guest passes to adjacent athletic club.

L ocated 22 miles south of Seattle and 10 miles north of Tacoma, the Federal Way Executel – Best Western offers visitors their choice of comfortable guest rooms or spacious suites. All rooms feature complimentary in-room coffeemakers, HBO with additional premium channels and data ports. Guest can enjoy the seasonal heated outdoor pool and hot tub or take advantage of free passes to the adjacent athletic club.

The Executel is within walking distance of the Sea-Tac Mall, theaters and restaurants. Within a 10-mile radius are the SuperMall, golf courses, state parks with marinas and hiking trails, Enchanted Park and many more family fun activities.

South Fork Moorage – Guest Houseboats

South Fork Moorage – Guest Houseboats
2187 Mann Road
Fir Island, Washington 98238
(360) 445-4803

Room Rates: $80 – $115.
Pet Charges or Deposits: None. Small pets only. Manager's approval required.
Rated: 4 Paws 🐾 🐾 🐾 🐾   2 nonsmoking houseboats for up to 4 guests, each with a fully
                         equipped galley, wood-burning stove, barbecue, front and back
                         decks.

F loating in a quiet cove on the Skagit River are the South Fork Moorage – Guest Houseboats. Spend some time relaxing on the deck as the magic of the river and the gentle movements of a charming houseboat lull your worries away.

These unique, cozy houseboats are moored off the coast of Fir Island. Each houseboat has a fully equipped kitchen, separate sleeping areas, a cozy wood-burning stove and wonderful observation decks.

Drop your line off the deck and try your hand at catching dinner, or venture out onto the river for canoeing, boating or swimming. There are spectacular fields on the island, which offer a blaze of color from tulips in the spring.

Kalaloch Lodge

Kalaloch Lodge
157151 Highway 101
Forks, Washington 98331
(360) 962-2271

Room Rates:	$99 – $200.
Pet Charges or Deposits:	$10 per day. First night's room rate as deposit.
Rated: 4 Paws 🐾🐾🐾🐾	58 guest rooms and 2 suites, some with ocean views, fireplaces, kitchens.

P erched on a bluff overlooking the Pacific Ocean sits one of the most memorable resorts in Olympic National Park. It's Kalaloch Lodge, and it has the charming characteristics of an oceanside fishing village.

Here you'll discover cozy oceanfront log cabins with Franklin fireplaces, and charming guest rooms that suit any vacationer's lifestyle.

There are plenty of activities to keep you busy, with hiking, fishing, clamming, beachcombing and exploring the endless tidepools. Since the lodge is located within a national park, leash laws do apply.

Inn at Friday Harbor

Inn at Friday Harbor
410 Spring Street
P.O. Box 339
Friday Harbor, Washington 98250
800-752-5752 • (360) 378-3031

Room Rates:	$59 – $234. AAA and AARP discounts.
Pet Charges or Deposits:	$50 refundable deposit.
Rated: 3 Paws 🐾🐾🐾	72 guest rooms, kitchenettes, room service, laundry facilities, exercise room, sauna, Jacuzzi, heated indoor swimming pool and restaurant.

T he San Juan Islands, home of the Inn at Friday Harbor, are a peaceful, breathtakingly beautiful natural paradise surrounded by crystal-clear waters and snow-capped mountains.

Select a spacious guest room or suite accommodations with a separate living room, fully equipped kitchen and patio or deck. You can swim year-round in the Inn's indoor pool and enjoy using the spa, sauna and exercise room.

Tucker House Bed and Breakfast with Cottages

Tucker House Bed and Breakfast with Cottages
260 B Street
Friday Harbor, Washington 98250
800-965-0123 • (360) 378-2783

Room Rates:	$75 – $210, including full breakfast.
Pet Charges or Deposits:	$15 per day. $15 nonrefundable deposit. Manager's approval required. Small dogs only. Sorry, no cats.
Rated: 4 Paws 🐾 🐾 🐾 🐾	2 bed-and-breakfast rooms with shared bath, wraparound porch and lovely gardens, plus 3 private cottages with full baths, kitchenettes, wood-burning stoves, electric heaters and sun decks; outdoor hot tub for all guests.

Built in 1898, the Tucker House Bed and Breakfast with Cottages is a charming Victorian home has been turned into a bed and breakfast. Upstairs are two bedrooms decorated in antiques, with queen-sized beds and a shared bath.

Three private cottages offer queen-sized beds, kitchenettes, wood-burning stoves and large sun decks. Each morning a full breakfast is served for all guests in the solarium of the main house. Their signature dish is their famous home-made cinnamon bread.

The State Ferry Landing and the waterfront are only two blocks from the Tucker House Bed and Breakfast with Cottages.

West Winds Harmony Cottage

West Winds Harmony Cottage
685 Spring Street, No. 107
Friday Harbor, Washington 98250
(360) 378-5283
Web Site: www.karuna.com/westwinds

Room Rates:	$150 – $225.
Pet Charges or Deposits:	None.
Rated: 4 Paws 🐾 🐾 🐾 🐾	Private one-bedroom, one-bath, two-story cottage for up to four, with extra queen-sized bed downstairs in living room, full kitchen, wood-burning stove, covered decks, views of the mountains and water.

Four wooded acres with views of the Strait of Juan de Fuca, summer residence for hundreds of orca whales, is the setting for West Winds Harmony Cottage. This private one-bedroom, two-story cottage sleeps up to four with the extra queen-sized bed downstairs in the living room.

Harmony Cottage has a fireplace and a fully equipped kitchen. French doors open onto the covered deck surrounding the entire house — wonderful for outside dining.

The Orca Whale Watch Park is a mile down the coastline — a lovely morning walk with a chance to see eagles perched in trees, ready to swoop down for their salmon breakfast. This enchanting cottage offers complete tranquillity for mind and spirit. The sunsets over the water are extraordinary.

Wharfside Bed and Breakfast Aboard the "Jacquelyn"

Wharfside Bed and Breakfast Aboard the "Jacquelyn"
Slip K-13, Port of Friday Harbor
Mailing address:
P.O. Box 1212
Friday Harbor, Washington 98250
(360) 378-5661

Room Rates:	$90 – $95, including full breakfast.
Pet Charges or Deposits:	$10 per day.
Rated: 4 Paws 🐾🐾🐾🐾	2 guest staterooms, sky-lit main salon with wood-burning fireplace.

A summer island adventure or a romantic winter retreat is yours aboard the "Jacquelyn," docked in Port of Friday Harbor. This 60-foot, ketch-rigged motorsailer is fully seaworthy, but remains docked as a year-round floating bed-and-breakfast inn.

On board are two spacious, private staterooms with elegant hardwoods, double and queen-sized beds with down comforters, dual-control mattress warmers, electric heaters and private full baths. There is a special area near the dock for your dog to get its daily exercise.

The sky-lit main salon is furnished with antiques and art, warmed by a wood-burning fireplace. Each morning a sumptuous array of breakfast specialties are freshly prepared in the galley.

Alta Crystal Resort

Alta Crystal Resort
68317 State Route 410 East
Greenwater, Washington 98022
800-277-6475 • (360) 663-2500

Room Rates:	$89 – $179.
Pet Charges or Deposits:	$15 per day. Manager's approval required.
Rated: 5 Paws	25 chalets and cabins on 22 acres, with fully equipped kitchens, wood stoves or fireplaces, outdoor hot tub, swimming pool and recreation area.

L ocated near the entrance to Mount Rainier National Park and the Crystal Mountain ski area, Alta Crystal Resort is the perfect choice for a group retreat, family vacation or ski trip.

The spacious log cabins and chalets offer wood-burning stoves or fireplaces and fully equipped kitchens, complete with all the modern appliances.

With a creek, a pond, hiking trails and 22 acres of woods and open fields, you and your dog will have plenty of room to explore. Resident dogs Beta Max and Fortuna, the co-managers of the property, will show your dog all their favorite places.

Howard Johnson Inn

Howard Johnson Inn
1233 North Central
Kent, Washington 98032
800-446-4656 • (253) 852-7224

Room Rates:	$63 – $96, including continental breakfast. AAA and AARP discounts.
Pet Charges or Deposits:	$25 refundable deposit.
Rated: 3 Paws 🐾 🐾 🐾	85 guest rooms and 1 suite, heated outdoor swimming pool, whirlpool spa, sauna, exercise room, laundry facilities.

entrally located between Seattle and Tacoma, the Howard Johnson Inn offers business travelers and families on vacation comfortable accommodations at reasonable rates. Guests will appreciate the convenient location of the inn when visiting this area. You are only minutes from the Boeing and Seattle International Raceways and the Green River Valley, as well as area stores and antique shops.

There are numerous city, state and national parks nearby, such as Dash Point State Park, a 397-acre park located five miles outside of Tacoma. If you are looking for water sports, visit Kopachuck State Park, a 127-acre park located sixteen miles west of Tacoma, where you will find scuba diving, water-skiing, boating, fishing, hiking trails and picnic areas.

La Quinta Inn

La Quinta Inn
10530 Northeast Northup Way
Kirkland, Washington 98033
800-687-6667 • (425) 828-6585

Room Rates:	$85 – $155, including a deluxe continental breakfast.
Pet Charges or Deposits:	$20 refundable deposit. Manager's approval required.
Rated: 3 Paws	122 guest rooms, heated swimming pool, spa, health club privileges.

L ocated near many of the major businesses, the University of Washington and area attractions, the spacious rooms, oversized bathrooms and large work areas make this Inn a good choice.

Start your day with the complimentary breakfast featuring cereal, fresh fruit, bagels, pastries, juice and freshly brewed coffee. Free health club passes are included in your room rate, along with the added enjoyment of the heated swimming pool and spa on the property.

Country Inn

Country Inn
107 South Second Street
La Conner, Washington 98257
(360) 466-3101

Room Rates: $93 – $117, including continental breakfast.
Pet Charges or Deposits: $25, plus credit card as deposit.
Rated: 4 Paws 🐾🐾🐾🐾   28 guest rooms.

T ucked away on the Swinomish Channel, in the farming and fishing community of Skagit Valley, is the home of the Country Inn. This cozy inn welcomes you with comfortable rooms, each with a fireplace and all the modern amenities you would expect to find in a luxury inn. Your complimentary breakfast is served each morning in the library.

The history and charm of La Conner is evident, from the Victorian houses with their widow's walks, to the unique shops and restaurants and the artists' center with authentic Indian crafts. Be sure to take in all the town's landmarks, such as the picturesque Rainbow Bridge.

Der Ritterhof Motor Inn

Der Ritterhof Motor Inn
190 U.S. Highway 2
P.O. Box 307
Leavenworth, Washington 98826
800-255-5845 • (509) 548-5845

Room Rates:	$70 – $140. AAA and AARP discounts.
Pet Charges or Deposits:	None.
Rated: 3 Paws 🐾🐾🐾	53 guest rooms and 3 suites, some with kitchenettes, hot tubs, heated swimming pool, children's play area and putting green.

ocated in the charming village of Leavenworth is Der Ritterhof Motor Inn. Designed in true Bavarian style, the Inn offers guests a wide range of comfortable accommodations and suites.

Leavenworth is known for its year-round recreation activities. The scenic Tumwater Canyon, with the Wenatchee River flowing through it, blazes with color in the fall and is one of the most popular areas for fishing and river-rafting in the state.

For those who wish to stay close to the Inn, there are plenty of activities as well. The heated swimming pool and hot tub are a wonderful diversion while the kids are enjoying the children's play area. A putting green, horseshoes, volleyball and badminton are available as well.

College Way Inn – Best Western

College Way Inn – Best Western
300 West College Way
Mount Vernon, Washington 98273
800-793-4024 • (360) 424-4287

Room Rates:	$48 – $78, including continental breakfast. AAA, AARP, AKC and ABA discounts.
Pet Charges or Deposits:	$5 per stay.
Rated: 3 Paws 🐾🐾🐾	66 guest rooms and 6 suites with lanais or balconies, some kitchenettes, heated swimming pool and whirlpool.

 he exquisite Mount Vernon area has long been known for its scenic fields of daffodils and tulips in spring and as home of the College Way Inn – Best Western.

The Inn offers comfortable accommodations, including many rooms with kitchenettes, at an affordable rate that includes a continental breakfast. The staff even has tasty dog biscuits for your dog.

CottonTree Inn – Best Western

CottonTree Inn – Best Western
2300 Market Street
Mount Vernon, Washington 98273
800-662-6886 • (360) 428-5678

Room Rates:	$69 – $89, including continental breakfast. AAA and AARP discounts.
Pet Charges or Deposits:	$10 per stay. Small pets only.
Rated: 3 Paws 🐾 🐾 🐾	121 guest rooms and suites, seasonally heated swimming pool, adjacent health club, restaurant and cocktail lounge.

L ocated midway between the cosmopolitan lifestyles of Seattle and Vancouver, yet surrounded by the natural beauty of the Cascade Mountains, is the CottonTree Inn. You will find all the modern conveniences such as valet laundry, an adjacent health club for your workout and a seasonally heated swimming pool.

Located near the Skagit River, the area is known for its quaint charm, unique shops, abundant wildlife and unmatched natural beauty. There is plenty of open space, with neighborhood, state and national parks for you and your dog to explore.

Harbor Pointe Bed and Breakfast

Harbor Pointe Bed and Breakfast
1486 Bonnie View Acres Road
Oak Harbor, Washington 98277
800-668-1110 • (360) 675-3379

Room Rates:	$85 – $150, including full breakfast.
Pet Charges or Deposits:	$25 per stay, plus first night's room rate as deposit. Manager's approval required.
Rated: 3 Paws	2 guest rooms and 3 suites, all with private baths, some with private entrances, decks, refrigerators and microwaves.

Spend your day searching out the treasures of Whidbey Island, walk the private beach or just put your feet up and relax in the spacious, high-beamed, cedar-lined living area with panoramic water views, surrounded with natural beauty.

What makes this very private bed and breakfast stand out from the crowd is the peaceful and relaxing ambiance that has been created, along with the superior accommodations. Relax in the large hot tub, while watching eagles soar and sailboats glide into Oak Harbor's sheltered haven.

Guest rooms are elegant and comfortable, with soft feather comforters, Amish sleigh beds, color cable TV and VCR and private decks and balconies with views. Awaken to a full breakfast "fit for a king" each morning.

Sunset View Resort

Sunset View Resort
P.O. Box 399
Ocean Park, Washington 98640
800-272-9199 • (360) 665-4494

Room Rates:	$65 – $185. AAA and AARP discounts.
Pet Charges or Deposits:	$10 per stay. Manager's approval required.
Rated: 3 Paws 🐾🐾🐾	42 guest rooms and 10 suites, hot tubs and sauna, beach, picnic/barbecue area and children's playground.

xperience the rare beauty of pristine forests, breathtaking sunsets and seemingly endless beaches at Sunset View Resort. Located on the Long Beach Peninsula, this resort is a good choice for a weekend retreat or a family vacation.

Take time to explore the area's wildlife at the Leadbetter State Park Wildlife Sanctuary located nearby. Afterward, indulge yourself with a soak in the hot tub or relax in the sauna. The resort also has a picnic and barbecue area, a playground for the children, croquet, volleyball, tennis, basketball, tetherball, horseshoes and a firepit so you can stay out and enjoy those incredible sunsets.

Olalla Orchard Bed and Breakfast

Olalla Orchard Bed and Breakfast
12530 Orchard Avenue Southeast
Olalla, Washington 98359
(253) 857-5915

Room Rates:	$95, including full breakfast.
Pet Charges or Deposits:	None.
Rated: 3 Paws 🐾🐾🐾	2 nonsmoking guest rooms with whirlpool tub, living room and dining areas, large porch and mountain views.

L ocated in the scenic Olalla Valley on three park-like acres, surrounded by small farms, country homes and pasture lands, is the Olalla Orchard Bed and Breakfast. This private home features large guest rooms with a private, two-person whirlpool bath and a porch that overlooks the property. Views of Mount Rainier are seen from the living and dining rooms.

Activities include dining and shopping in Gig Harbor, a country walk or bicycle ride, a picnic on one of the nearby beaches, a boat launch into nearby Colvos Passage (part of Puget Sound), fishing off the Olalla Bridge or just a weekend getaway.

Cinnamon Rabbit Bed and Breakfast

Cinnamon Rabbit Bed and Breakfast
1304 Seventh Avenue West
Olympia, Washington 98502
(360) 357-5520

Room Rates: $55 – $80, including full breakfast.
Pet Charges or Deposits: None. Small pets only. Manager's approval required.
Rated: 3 Paws 🐾 🐾 🐾   2 guest rooms, hot tub, spacious grounds with organic garden, walking distance to beach.

 Built in 1935, on the southern end of Puget Sound, this Dutch Colonial-style home offers guests their choice of two cozy bedrooms. The lovely grounds are edged in flowers and include an organic vegetable garden.

In the morning you are treated to a breakfast featuring delicious homemade waffles with fresh blueberries and raspberries. Low-fat or vegetarian meals can be prepared — just ask your hosts and they will gladly oblige.

For those who are feeling adventurous, the beach is within walking distance, as is Capitol Lake Park. The area also offers canoeing, white-water rafting, golf, swimming, tennis, mountain biking and hiking. Located within driving distance are historic sights, several antique shops, the aquarium, nature areas, vineyards and Olympic National Forest, where you and your dog can explore more than 632,000 acres of parkland.

Puget View Guesthouse

Puget View Guesthouse
7924 61st Avenue Northeast
Olympia, Washington 98516
(360) 413-9474

Room Rates:	$89, including deluxe continental breakfast.
Pet Charges or Deposits:	$10 per day. Manager's approval required.
Rated: 4 Paws	A private two-room guest cottage, deluxe continental breakfast served at your door, deck with barbecue, ocean and mountain views.

P uget View Guesthouse is a secluded cottage on the shore of Puget Sound. Since 1984, guests have come to appreciate its peaceful beauty and comfortable hospitality. Tall firs, Olympic Mountains and island views surround you in this 1930s log house.

The cottage interior is complete with queen-sized bed, private bath, sitting room with sofa sleeper, dining area, refrigerator and microwave. A "continental plus" breakfast is served at your door. Outside, enjoy your deck and barbecue, lounge in the hammock or walk the beach.

Cedar House Inn Bed and Breakfast

Cedar House Inn Bed and Breakfast
1534 Gulf Road
Point Roberts, Washington 98281
(360) 945-0284

Room Rates:	$36 – $49, including full breakfast.
Pet Charges or Deposits:	$10 refundable deposit.
Rated: 3 Paws	6 guest rooms, laundry facilities, views of the Georgia Strait and the mountains.

L ocated on the tiny peninsula of Point Roberts, only one mile from the Canadian border, is the Cedar House Inn Bed and Breakfast, the closest U.S. lodging to Vancouver.

This unique 3,800-square-foot home has a large living-dining room combination, where you will enjoy your country breakfast each morning, a floor-to-ceiling brick fireplace, cathedral ceilings and a wall of windows from which to view the waves off the Georgia Strait and the picturesque mountains. Guests can choose from six comfortable guest rooms with king- or queen-sized beds.

When visiting this area you will want to explore the natural beauty of the wooded hiking paths that cut through the giant cedar trees, pick wildflowers and blackberries when in season, visit the coast's largest heron rookery, go fishing or boating or simply roam the beach with your dog.

DoubleTree Hotel

DoubleTree Hotel
221 North Lincoln Street
Port Angeles, Washington 98362
800-222-TREE • (360) 452-9215
Web Site: www.doubletreehotels.com

Room Rates:	$69 – $119, including full breakfast. AAA and AARP discounts.
Pet Charges or Deposits:	$30 refundable deposit. Small pets only.
Rated: 3 Paws 🐾🐾🐾	184 guest rooms and 3 suites, some with refrigerators; heated swimming pool, whirlpool, room service, dining room and coffee shop.

On the Strait of Juan de Fuca, one block from the center of town and from the ferry to Victoria, British Columbia, is the DoubleTree Hotel. This waterfront hotel offers guests spacious accommodations with balconies overlooking the harbor. You'll find all the services and amenities you'd expect of a first-class hotel, including laundry, valet and room service.

Here you will find a heated swimming pool, a relaxing hot tub, a city jogging trail running in front of the hotel and a small beach, perfect for an outing with your dog. Local attractions abound, with visits to rain forests, ocean beaches, natural hot springs, Olympic National Park, Hurricane Ridge, the Olympic Game Farm, Neah Bay, Lake Crescent and Ediz Hook Harbor, all located within minutes of the hotel.

Log Cabin Resort

Log Cabin Resort
3183 East Beach Road
Port Angeles, Washington 98363
(360) 928-3325

Room Rates:	$48 – $119.
Pet Charges or Deposits:	$6 per day.
Rated: 3 Paws 🐾 🐾 🐾	28 lakeside lodge rooms and rustic cabins, restaurant and general store.

Y ou'll be secluded among giant old-growth firs and cedars, with nearby trails to spectacular waterfalls, snow-capped mountains and the deep blue water of Lake Crescent. To the south, Mount Storm King rises above the lake. This popular vacation and recreation paradise displays the variety for which Olympic National Park is so famous.

The resort offers a variety of accommodations: lakeside chalets, comfortable lodge rooms and rustic cabins, as well as full hookup RV sites.

Whatever you like to do — hiking, boating, water sports, or just a lakeside picnic — you'll find it here, in a picturesque environment. Or try your luck fishing for the elusive Beardslee trout, the ultimate Northwest trophy.

Maple Rose Inn

Maple Rose Inn
112 Reservoir Road
Port Angeles, Washington 98363
800-570-2007 • (360) 457-ROSE
Web Site: www.northolymic.com/maplerose
E-mail: maplerose@tenforward.com

Room Rates:	$79 – $147, including full country breakfast.
Pet Charges or Deposits:	$15. Manager's approval required.
Rated: 3 Paws	2 guest rooms and 3 suites, Jacuzzis, kitchenettes and private decks.

T he Maple Rose Inn, a contemporary bed and breakfast, offers a serene setting in the foothills of the Olympic Mountains. Spacious common areas offer guests the opportunity to relax with a book or view a movie. You can take tea in the solarium, use the exercise facilities, soak in the hot tub, or unwind on the deck.

Popular nearby activities include cross-country skiing at Hurricane Ridge, hiking or snowshoeing to the Sol Duc Hot Springs, exploring nature and viewing wildlife on the world-famous Dungeness Spit, and biking along scenic countryside roads. Olympic National Park is literally in the front yard of the Inn, offering trails to explore with your dog.

Inn at Ludlow Bay

Inn at Ludlow Bay
One Heron Road
Port Ludlow, Washington 98365
(360) 437-0411

Room Rates: $138 – $450, including continental breakfast.
Pet Charges or Deposits: $50 refundable deposit. Manager's approval required.
Rated: 4 Paws 🐾 🐾 🐾 🐾   34 spacious rooms and 3 suites, ocean views, fireplaces, over-
                         sized Jacuzzi tubs, boat moorage at marina, waterfront dining
                         and fireside bar.

L ocated on a finger of the Olympic Peninsula on the Hood Canal is the Inn at Ludlow Bay. Here guests are surrounded by spectacular views of the waterfront and the picturesque Olympic and Cascade Mountains.

Guest rooms offer scenic views, fireplaces, oversized Jacuzzi tubs, plush terrycloth bathrobes and comfortable beds with down-filled comforters. For those arriving at the Inn by boat, priority boat moorage can be arranged at Port Ludlow Marina.

The sandy shores surrounding the inn are perfect for beachcombing, fishing, boating or kayaking in the Hood Canal. The scenic array of state parks is perfect for day excursions, hiking, mountain biking and sightseeing.

Palace Hotel

Palace Hotel
1004 Water Street
Port Townsend, Washington 98368
800-962-0741 • (360) 385-0773
Web Site: www.olympus.net/palace
E-mail: palace@olympus.net

Room Rates:	$59 – $139, including continental breakfast. AAA, AARP, AKC and ABA discounts.
Pet Charges or Deposits:	$20 per stay.
Rated: 4 Paws 🐾🐾🐾🐾	13 guest rooms and 3 suites, fireplaces, Jacuzzi or clawfoot tubs, efficiencies and kitchens, laundry facilities, restaurant.

T he historic town of Port Townsend to home for the charming 1889 Victorian-style Palace Hotel. Each spacious guest room in this beautifully restored hotel is uniquely decorated in a Victorian theme and furnished in period antiques.

Many of the rooms have views of Port Townsend Bay or historic downtown and offer Jacuzzi or old-fashioned clawfoot tubs and cozy fireplaces. Guests are treated to a continental breakfast of fresh pastries and fruit delivered to their room each morning.

Swan Hotel and Conference Center

Swan Hotel and Conference Center
Monroe and Water Streets
Port Townsend, Washington 98368
800-776-1718 • (360) 385-1718
Web Site: www.waypt.com/bishop
E-mail: swan@wapt.com

Room Rates:	$79 – $129, including continental breakfast. AAA, AARP, AKC and ABA discounts.
Pet Charges or Deposits:	$10 per pet, per day.
Rated: 4 Paws 🐾🐾🐾🐾	2 penthouses, 4 suites and 4 studio cottages, kitchenettes.

T he Swan Hotel, located in the historic downtown district, offers visitors downtown convenience in newly redecorated condominium-style suites and cottages.

The one-bedroom suites feature queen-sized beds, full baths with tubs, living rooms with cable TV and queen-sized sofas that convert into beds. Each suite offers a kitchenette with a dining table and chairs, distinctively furnished with fine marine art and antiques. Decks offer views of the Straits of Juan De Fuca and Admiralty Inlet.

The penthouses occupy the top two floors of the main building, with decks offering unparalleled views of the Cascade and Olympic mountains.

Adjacent to the main building are four "historic" cottages, newly remodeled with hardwood floors, new built-in queen-sized beds, full bathrooms and kitchenettes.

Heritage Inn – Best Western

Heritage Inn – Best Western
928 Northwest Olsen Street
Pullman, Washington 99163
800-528-1234 • (509) 332-0928

Room Rates:	$59 – $159, including continental breakfast and evening snacks. AAA and AARP discounts.
Pet Charges or Deposits:	None.
Rated: 3 Paws 🐾 🐾 🐾	59 guest rooms and 9 suites, mini-kitchens, room service, indoor swimming pool, spa and sauna.

C onveniently located in Pullman, near Washington State University, is the Heritage Inn – Best Western. Guests will find a variety of guest rooms and spa suites with king-sized beds, spa tubs and mini-kitchens.

To make your stay even more comfortable, the Inn offers complimentary evening cookies and popcorn to make you feel at home. Guests can enjoy the indoor swimming pool, spa and sauna any time of the day or night.

Holiday Inn Express

Holiday Inn Express
1190 Bishop Boulevard Southeast
Pullman, Washington 99163
800-HOLIDAY • (509) 334-4437

Room Rates:	$79 – $99, including continental breakfast and bedtime snacks. AAA and AARP discounts.
Pet Charges or Deposits:	None.
Rated: 3 Paws 🐾 🐾 🐾	116 guest rooms and 14 suites, some with kitchenettes, heated indoor swimming pool, whirlpool, exercise room, seasonal outdoor sports court, laundry facilities, rental bicycles and a "pet park" area.

T here are several room types to choose from, offering whirlpool tubs and wet bars with microwaves and refrigerators. Ample parking, guest laundry facilities, dry-cleaning services and a business center are all available for your convenience.

The indoor swimming pool with its wave jets and whirlpool spa are enjoyed by guests year-round, along with the fitness room and outdoor recreation area, where you may play games such as volleyball and croquet. Both you and your pet will appreciate the special "pet park," an area set aside for guests to exercise their pets.

The inn is a favorite for guests who are bringing their pets to the famous Washington State University Veterinary Hospital, conveniently located only one mile from the inn.

Lake Quinault Lodge

Lake Quinault Lodge
345 South Shore Road
P.O. Box 7
Quinault, Washington 98575
800-562-6672 (Oregon & Washington only) • (360) 288-2900

Room Rates:	$65 – $140. AAA, AARP and seasonal discounts.
Pet Charges or Deposits:	$10 per pet, per day.
Rated: 4 Paws 🐾 🐾 🐾 🐾	92 guest rooms with fireplaces, lake or mountain views, restaurant and cocktail lounge.

estled in the heart of Olympic National Forest lies a sanctuary with a sweeping view of a pristine lake, known as Lake Quinault Lodge. Built in 1926, the lodge is set on Lake Quinault, with the Olympic Mountains in the background.

Tastefully appointed guest rooms offer a restful retreat for those visiting the Northwest. The heated indoor pool and dry sauna are a great diversion after a day of hiking, canoeing, sea cycling or any of the other outdoor activities at the lodge.

The Roosevelt Dining Room, with its Native American art decor, features a savory selection of Northwest regional cuisine.

Hanford House – DoubleTree Hotel

Hanford House – DoubleTree Hotel
802 George Washington Way
Richland, Washington 99352
800-222-TREE • (509) 946-7611

Room Rates: $47 – $119; some rates include full breakfast.
Pet Charges or Deposits: None. No large dogs, please.
Rated: 3 Paws 🐾🐾🐾   150 guest rooms and 7 suites, some with river views,
                          refrigerators, balconies or patios; heated swimming pool,
                          whirlpool, boat dock, health club privileges, 24-hour room
                          service, restaurant and cocktail lounge.

On the banks of the Columbia River you will find spacious guest rooms and luxury suites with scenic views of the river and surrounding area. The river setting is perfect for those traveling with pets. You and your four-legged companion won't have to venture far to find a place to play, with Howard Amon Park located directly behind the hotel.

Do a few laps in the swimming pool or loosen up in the hot tub. The courtyard offers badminton and volleyball. Nearby, you'll find boat rentals, tennis, nine golf courses, jogging and shopping.

Heritage Inn – Best Western

Heritage Inn – Best Western
1513 Smitty's Boulevard
Ritzville, Washington 99169
800-528-1234 • (509) 659-1007

Room Rates:	$49 – $149, including continental breakfast and evening snacks. AAA and AARP discounts.
Pet Charges or Deposits:	None.
Rated: 3 Paws 🐾🐾🐾	42 guest rooms and 2 spa suites, kitchenettes, heated swimming pool, whirlpool and laundry facilities.

 omfort and convenience are the No. 1 priority at this 3 Diamond, AAA-rated inn. Your room rate includes a deluxe continental breakfast of freshly made muffins, bagels, yogurt, fresh fruit, juice, hot coffee and tea. In the evening you will find homemade cookies, hot spiced cider and lemonade in the lobby.

The Heritage Inn – Best Western offers a heated outdoor swimming pool and hot tub area for guests to enjoy.

Alexis Hotel

Alexis Hotel
1007 First Avenue
Seattle, Washington 98104
800-426-7033 • (206) 624-4433

Room Rates: $210 – $550, including evening wine-tasting.
Pet Charges or Deposits: None.
Rated: 5 Paws 66 guest rooms and 43 suites, kitchens, 2 tennis courts, exercise and spa facilities, steam room, whirlpool, 24-hour room service, restaurant and cocktail lounge.

L ocated in downtown Seattle, the Alexis Hotel, has elegantly welcomed guests from around the world since 1901. Its graceful refinement and warm hospitality make it a premier hotel.

The guest rooms are warm and rich, with an eclectic mix of tradition highlighted by a scattering of antiques. Some of the elegant, spacious suites feature wood-burning fireplaces, jetted tubs and graciously appointed sitting and dining rooms, perfect for the discriminating traveler.

At the Alexis you can expect the red-carpet treatment for both you and your pet. This "pet friendly" hotel has always welcomed pets, but they go out of their way to assure that "all" of their guests have an enjoyable stay. In their opinion, bringing your pet makes the hotel feel more like home. So when you call for room service, be sure to add a doggy bone for Fido or a saucer of warm milk for Fluffy to your order.

Four Seasons Olympic Hotel

Four Seasons Olympic Hotel
411 University Street
Seattle, Washington 98101
800-223-8772 • (206) 621-1700

Room Rates: $295 – $365.
Pet Charges or Deposits: None.
Rated: 5 Paws 🐾🐾🐾🐾🐾 450 guest rooms and suites, fully equipped health club with pool, whirlpool, sauna and massage, three restaurants.

 ovingly restored to its 1924 Italian Renaissance glory, the Four Seasons Olympic Hotel reflects the splendor of another age. Here you will enjoy the comfort and elegance of the city's most spacious accommodations, all conveniently close to the key cultural, business and retail centers.

Each year the hotel wins top national and international honors from the lodging industry for its superb service and state-of-the-art restaurants. The Four Seasons Olympic Hotel also offers some of the city's best shopping, featuring more than a dozen exclusive salons and luxury retail shops. The hotel is within minutes of the Fifth Avenue Theater, Seattle Art Museum, Pike Place Market and the waterfront.

Guests of the hotel can maintain their exercise regimens in the on-site health club, which includes a lap pool and cardiovascular equipment.

Residence Inn by Marriott – Fairview Avenue North

Residence Inn by Marriott – Fairview Avenue North
800 Fairview Avenue North
Seattle, Washington 98109
(206) 624-6000

Room Rates:	$110 — $290, including continental breakfast. AAA and AARP discounts.
Pet Charges or Deposits:	$10 per pet, per day. Call for deposit requirements.
Rated: 4 Paws 🐾🐾🐾🐾	234 studio, one- and two-bedroom suites, with fully equipped kitchens, some balconies with river views, indoor lap pool, spa, steam room, sauna and exercise facilities.

Along the banks of Lake Union, the Residence Inn by Marriott offers visitors to the Seattle area the comfort and conveniences of home. Residence Inn is designed with a residential look and feel, from the inside out.

Choose from a studio or a one- or two-bedroom suite with fully equipped kitchen, a spacious, elegantly appointed living area and views of the lake.

Each morning a buffet-style breakfast awaits you by the waterfall in the seven-story garden atrium lobby. Unwind with a swim in the pool, relax in the heated spa, or hit the Sport Court for a game of racquet sports, basketball or volleyball.

Salish Lodge and Spa

Salish Lodge and Spa
6501 Railroad Avenue Southeast
P.O. Box 1109
Snoqualmie, Washington 98065
800-826-6124 • (206) 888-2556
Web Site: www.salish.com

Room Rates: $169 – $269. AAA discount.
Pet Charges or Deposits: $50 per stay. Manager's approval required.
Rated: 5 Paws 😺 😺 😺 😺 😺 90 guest rooms and 4 suites, complete spa facilities, rooftop
                       hot tub, heated therapy pools and restaurant.

S et in the middle of the Snoqualmie Valley, the Salish Lodge and Spa blends naturally into its surroundings. This harmonious fusion of the rustic and the sophisticated assures guests absolute comfort. You'll enjoy Four Diamond luxury enhanced by the spectacular sights and sounds of Snoqualmie Falls.

Every well-appointed guest room has a wood-burning fireplace, an oversized whirlpool tub, custom designed furniture, pillowed window seats and fluffy goose-down comforters. Spend a day in the tranquil spa, featuring massage, aromatherapy and skin and body renewal treatments. The rooftop hot tub is perfect for gazing at the stars and feeling as if there is no one else in the world.

The only thing that could possibly compare with the picturesque scenery surrounding the lodge is the fabulous cuisine. From breakfast to dinner, the culinary brilliance is evident.

A Spokane Bed and Breakfast Service

A Spokane Bed and Breakfast Service
East 627 – 25th
Spokane, Washington 99203
888-626-3776 • (509) 624-3776

Room Rates: $45 – $105, including full or continental breakfast.
Pet Charges or Deposits: None. Manager's approval required. Sorry, no cats.
Rated: 3 Paws 🐾 🐾 🐾

 Bed and breakfasts are a time-honored alternative to conventional hotel/motel lodging. At A Spokane Bed and Breakfast Service they will personally select a bed and breakfast home to accommodate your needs.

These private homes feature comfortable guest rooms and common areas. If you enjoy gardens, dogs, good food and quality surroundings, you will enjoy these accommodations.

Awake each morning to a full breakfast on a large terrace overlooking the garden. Parks are only half a block away, offering tennis courts, exercise stops and paths for walking.

Cavanaugh's River Inn

Cavanaugh's River Inn
700 North Division Street
Spokane, Washington 99202
800-THE-INNS • (509) 326-5577
Web Site: www.cavanaughs.com

Room Rates:	$75 – $225. AAA and AARP discounts.
Pet Charges or Deposits:	None.
Rated: 3 Paws 🐾 🐾 🐾	245 guest rooms and 4 guest suites, pools, Jacuzzi, tennis courts and volleyball.

C avanaugh's River Inn is a full-service resort-style hotel located in a beautifully landscaped setting along the north bank of the Spokane River.

Superb hospitality and restful lodging at affordable prices are offered in tastefully appointed guest rooms and suites. Deluxe rooms feature king-sized beds, poolside access and river views.

Cavanaugh's offers two outdoor pools, one covered for year-round use, a children's wading pool, tennis and volleyball courts, a horseshoe pit and a children's playground. Enjoy a run along the two-mile loop path through Riverfront Park, then relax in the saunas and whirlpool. Access is convenient to the Centennial Trail across the river.

Thunderbird Inn – Best Western

Thunderbird Inn – Best Western
West 120 Third Avenue
Spokane, Washington 99204
800-578-2473 • (509) 747-2011

Room Rates:	$59 – $84, including continental breakfast. AAA and AARP discounts.
Pet Charges or Deposits:	$15 per day. Small dogs only. Sorry, no cats.
Rated: 3 Paws 🐾 🐾 🐾	89 guest rooms, some with refrigerators; heated swimming pool, whirlpool, exercise room and valet laundry.

L ocated in Spokane, the Thunderbird Inn – Best Western offers guests comfort and convenience at reasonable prices.

Each of the spacious guest rooms features a king-sized bed, comfortable recliner, in-room coffeemakers, modem outlets and dining/work areas, making it a good choice for the family on vacation or the traveling professional.

Convenient to freeway Exit 281, and all major thoroughfares, the Best Western Thunderbird Inn is only minutes from the Opera House, the Met Theater, Riverfront Park and the Spokane Arena.

Royal Coachman Inn

Royal Coachman Inn
5805 Pacific Highway East
Tacoma/Fife, Washington 98424
800-422-3051 • (253) 922-2500

Room Rates:	$65 – $125. AAA, AARP, AKC and ABA discounts.
Pet Charges or Deposits:	$25 refundable deposit.
Rated: 3 Paws 🐾🐾🐾	88 guest rooms and 6 suites, Jacuzzi and kitchenettes, laundry facilities, health club privileges, restaurant and cocktail lounge.

T he stone-covered exterior of the Royal Coachman Inn, with its medieval turrets, is located 20 minutes south of SeaTac Airport with easy access to Interstate 5.

Choose from a comfortable, spacious guest room or a suite offering all the comforts and conveniences of home. The Inn features a private library room with a cozy fireplace for meetings or large gatherings.

Health club privileges are available for guests of the Inn so you won't miss your daily workout while on vacation, and there is a whirlpool on the property.

Shilo Inn

Shilo Inn
7414 South Hosmer
Tacoma, Washington 98408
800-222-2244 • (206) 475-4020

Room Rates:	$79 – $95, including continental breakfast. AAA and AARP discounts.
Pet Charges or Deposits:	$7 per pet, per day.
Rated: 3 Paws 🐾 🐾 🐾	132 guest rooms and 2 suites, laundry facilities, jogging path, indoor swimming pool, spa, sauna, steam room and fitness center.

C onveniently located in the Tacoma/Fife area, the Shilo Inn offers guests comfortable accommodations at moderate prices.

Choose a standard room with a king-sized bed or two queen-sized beds, or a roomy suite or kitchen unit. A continental breakfast awaits you each morning.

The Inn's indoor swimming pool, spa, fitness center, sauna and steam room are available for guests to enjoy.

Llama Ranch Bed and Breakfast

Llama Ranch Bed and Breakfast
1980 Highway 141
Trout Lake, Washington 98650
(509) 395-2786

Room Rates:	$79 – $99, including full breakfast.
Pet Charges or Deposits:	None. Free boarding for your pet llama.
Rated: 3 Paws 🐾🐾🐾	5 guest rooms, laundry facilities.

I n a peaceful valley on a 97-acre ranch is the Llama Ranch Bed and Breakfast. Guests may choose from five private guest rooms with picturesque views of the ranch or the mountains.

One guest room has a king-sized bed and a queen-sized hide-a-bed, plus a private kitchen. Four other guest rooms, with queen-sized beds, which a common kitchen, living room, dining room and laundry facilities, making these accommodations the perfect choice for a private retreat for a small group or families with children. There are plenty of open spaces and wooded areas, allowing you and your dog to enjoy the great outdoors.

Guests of the ranch are treated to walks, hikes or even a picnic with the llamas. You will soon learn that besides their beauty and dignity, llamas' calm nature affects the people around them, producing a relaxing, serene atmosphere.

Alderbrook Resort

Alderbrook Resort
East 7101 Highway 106
Union, Washington 98592
800-622-9370 • (360) 898-2200

Room Rates:	$69 – $179. AAA and AARP discounts.
Pet Charges or Deposits:	$8 per day, plus $25 deposit.
Rated: 4 Paws 🐾🐾🐾🐾	18 housekeeping cottages, fully equipped kitchenettes, fireplaces and courtyards. Plus 80 guest rooms and 2 suites with private lanais and courtyards. Beachfront, heated indoor swimming pool, Jacuzzi, 4 tennis courts, marina and boat dock, playground, 18-hole golf course, restaurant and lounge.

 visit to Alderbrook Resort puts you in the midst of more than 525 wooded acres on the shores of beautiful Hood Canal, a fjord-like inlet of Puget Sound. Framed by the towering, snowcapped Olympic Mountains, Alderbrook Resort offers you unlimited recreation and fine accommodations.

No matter what your favorite recreation is, chances are you will find it here. Play tennis, relax in the heated indoor pool and Jacuzzi, bicycle or hike through the miles of forest and trails. Rent a pedal boat and tour the local area, or a power boat and water-ski the entire canal.

Guests have their choice of two-bedroom housekeeping cottages with fully equipped kitchenettes, brick fireplaces and private courtyards, or guest rooms and suites with private lanais.

Shilo Inn – Downtown

Shilo Inn – Downtown
401 East 13th Street
Vancouver, Washington 98660
800-222-2244 • (360) 696-0411

Room Rates:	$65 – $99, including continental breakfast. AAA and AARP discounts.
Pet Charges or Deposits:	$7 per pet, per day.
Rated: 3 Paws 🐾🐾🐾	118 guest rooms, some with microwaves and refrigerators; laundry facilities, seasonal heated swimming pool, indoor sauna, steam room, whirlpool, adjacent restaurant and cocktail lounge.

T he Inn offers guests comfortable, spacious, king-sized rooms with kitchenettes at economy rates. The Inn's "pet friendly" staff keeps dog biscuits and kitty treats on hand to make your pet feel welcome.

A continental breakfast is included in your room rate. Guests are encouraged to enjoy the pool, spa, steam room and sauna. Shilo Inn also offers free airport shuttles.

Shilo Inn – Hazel Dell

Shilo Inn – Hazel Dell
13206 Highway 99
Vancouver, Washington 98686
800-222-2244 • (360) 573-0511

Room Rates:	$65 – $85, including continental breakfast. AAA and AARP discounts.
Pet Charges or Deposits:	$7 per pet, per day.
Rated: 3 Paws 🐾🐾🐾	65 guest rooms, some kitchenettes, laundry facilities, heated indoor swimming pool, sauna, steam room and whirlpool.

H ere you will find comfortable guest accommodations featuring king-sized rooms and spacious kitchen units, perfect for extended stays or for the family on vacation, all at an affordable price. A continental breakfast is included in your room rate.

Guests are encouraged to enjoy the heated indoor swimming pool and whirlpool, steam room and sauna.

The nearby Columbia River Gorge National Scenic Area, located on the Oregon side of the river, offers a number of recreational activities. Enjoy more than 300,000 acres of parkland with waterfalls, forests and grassy plains.

Swallow's Nest Guest Cottages

Swallow's Nest Guest Cottages
6030 Southwest 248th Street
Vashon Island, Washington 98070
800-ANY-NEST • (206) 463-2646

Room Rates:	$75 – $170.
Pet Charges or Deposits:	$5 per pet, per day. Call for deposit requirements. Manager's approval required.
Rated: 4 Paws 🐾 🐾 🐾 🐾	5 private cottages with full kitchens, golf privileges, hot tub.

L ocated only a short ferry ride from Seattle, Tacoma, or the Olympic Peninsula, the Swallow's Nest Guest Cottages offer you a sojourn to a peaceful, country retreat at affordable rates.

Five charming cottages in three separate locations sit atop a bluff, looking out at Puget Sound, Mount Rainier and the Cascades. Large picture windows overlook orchards, pastures and the woods. The cottages are comfortably furnished with plants, televisions, cooking facilities, books, magazines and a supply of tea, cocoa and fresh coffee.

The community of Vashon offers kayaking, boating, fishing and swimming. The island has many good restaurants, antique shops, art galleries and parks to enjoy. Bicyclists will enjoy the miles of paved roads and outstanding views, which also provide a great way for you and your dog to explore the island.

Comfort Inn

Comfort Inn
520 North Second Avenue
Walla Walla, Washington 99362
800-228-5150 • (509) 525-2522

Room Rates:	$56 – $125, including continental breakfast and evening snacks. AAA and AARP discounts.
Pet Charges or Deposits:	None.
Rated: 3 Paws 🐾🐾🐾	61 guest rooms and 10 suites, kitchenettes, heated indoor swimming pool, spa, exercise room and laundry facilities.

hoose from a comfortable standard guest room with two double or queen-sized beds, a king-sized bed, or a Spa Suite with a king-sized bed in a large bedroom and a hide-a-bed sofa in the separate living room.

For long-term guests there are kitchen suites with queen- or king-sized beds, refrigerators, ranges and dishwashers. A deluxe continental breakfast is served in the lobby each morning, plus an evening snack of fresh-baked cookies, hot chocolate and freshly brewed coffee.

Located on the main floor you will find an indoor swimming pool and spa open 24 hours a day for you to enjoy. Your dog will appreciate the exercise area, where he can stretch his legs or play a game of catch.

Heritage Inn – Best Western

Heritage Inn – Best Western
1905 North Wenatchee Avenue
Wenatchee, Washington 98801
800-528-1234 • (509) 664-6565
E-mail: hospasoc@iea.com

Room Rates:	$63 – $135, including continental breakfast and evening snack. AAA and AARP discounts.
Pet Charges or Deposits:	None.
Rated: 3 Paws 🐾 🐾 🐾	65 rooms and 6 suites, kitchens and spas, heated indoor swimming pool, whirlpool, sauna and complimentary fitness center passes.

 et in the picturesque Wenatchee Valley, the Heritage Inn offers attractive guest rooms with microwave ovens and refrigerators.

Spacious suites feature full kitchens with all the needed utensils. The living/sleeping area has a queen-sized bed and a hide-a-bed sofa. In addition to the added convenience of in-room coffee, your room rate also includes a deluxe continental breakfast served in the lobby every morning, as well as complimentary fresh-baked cookies every evening. The Inn offers a pool, spa and sauna area for guests to enjoy 24 hours a day.

Cascade Inn – Best Western

Cascade Inn – Best Western
960 Highway 20
P.O. Box 813
Winthrop, Washington 98862
800-468-6754 • (509) 996-3100
E-mail: cascade@methow.com

Room Rates:	$50 – $125, including continental breakfast. AAA and AARP discounts.
Pet Charges or Deposits:	$10 per day, plus $10 nonrefundable deposit. Manager's approval required.
Rated: 3 Paws	63 guest rooms and 1 suite, heated swimming pool, hot tub, laundry facilities, picnic and barbecue area.

I n the heart of the scenic Methow Valley, near North Cascade National Park, is the Cascade Inn – Best Western. This riverfront property is conveniently located, offering comfortable accommodations at moderate prices.

After your complimentary continental breakfast, you can enjoy year-round outdoor recreation in one of the Northwest's most exciting four-season resort areas. Here you can play a round of golf, go river-rafting along the Columbia River, fishing at nearby Lake Chalan or Banks Lake, enjoy mountain biking, cross-country or downhill skiing, snowmobiling and horseback riding, all in one area.

If you are spending the day closer to the Inn, there is a hot tub for a relaxing soak, a heated swimming pool and a waterfall. Guests are encouraged to enjoy the barbecue and picnic area next to the river.

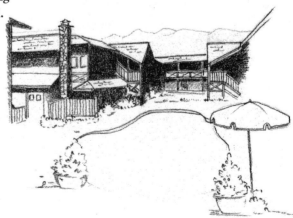

WHERE TO TAKE YOUR PETS IN
Washington

Please note: *Pets must be on a leash at all times and may be restricted to certain areas. For directions, use fees, pet charges and general information, contact the numbers listed below.*

National Forest and Parks General Information

Outdoor Recreation Information Office
915 Second Avenue, Room 442
Seattle, Washington 98174
(206) 220-7450
800-280-2267 or 365-2267 – information and reservations

National Forests

Gifford Pinchot National Forest, located in southwestern Washington, encompasses 1,299,546 acres of parkland consisting of mountains, meadows, caves, canyons and streams for you and your dog to explore. Enjoy the picnic areas, hiking and bicycle trails, a boat ramp, boat rentals, fishing, swimming, winter sports, mountain climbing, horse rentals and visitor's center. For more information, call (360) 750-5001.

Olympic National Forest is a 632,324-acre park located on the Olympic Peninsula in northwestern Washington. The park is known for its rugged mountain terrain, lush rain forests and glacial streams, with picnic areas, hiking and bicycle trails, a boat ramp, fishing, swimming, winter sports and visitor's center. For more information, call (360) 956-2400.

National Recreation Areas

Coulee Dam National Recreation Area, located along Franklin D. Roosevelt Lake toward the Canadian border in northwestern Washington, consists of 100,059 acres of parkland offering picnic areas, a boat ramp, boat rentals, fishing, swimming, water-skiing and a visitor's center. For more information, call (509) 633-9441.

State Parks General Information

State Parks and Recreation Commission
7150 Clearwater Lane
Olympia, Washington 98504
800-223-0321
(360) 902-8500

Department of Fish and Wildlife
600 Capitol Way North
Olympia, Washington 98501
(360) 902-2200

STATE PARKS

ANATONE

Fields Spring State Park, located 5 miles south of Anatone off State Route 129. The park offers picnic areas, hiking trails and winter sports such as snowmobiling.

BATTLE GROUND

Battle Ground Lake State Park is a 279-acre park located 3 miles northeast of Battle Ground off State Route 502, near Portland, Oregon. Visitors to the park will find picnic areas, hiking and bicycle trails, a boat ramp, fishing and swimming. For more information, call (360) 687-1510.

BELLINGHAM

Larrabee State Park encompasses 1,981 acres of parkland and is located 7 miles south of Bellingham on State Route 11. Visitors to the park will find picnic areas, hiking trails, a boat ramp, fishing, scuba diving and water-skiing.

BIRCH BAY

Birch Bay State Park, located 1 mile south of Birch Bay off State Route 548, is a 193-acre park offering areas for picnicking and fishing, plus hiking trails to explore with your dog.

BLACK DIAMOND

Flaming Geyser State Park encompasses 2,008 acres of parkland, located less than 2 miles south of Black Diamond on State Route 169, then continue west for 2.75 miles on Southeast Green Valley Road. Enjoy the picnic areas, hiking trails and fishing. For more information, call (206) 931-3930.

BOGACHIEL

Bogachiel State Park is a 119-acre park located 6 miles south of Forks at Bogachiel on U.S. Highway 101. Visitors to the park will find picnic areas, hiking trails, boating, boat rentals and fishing.

BREMERTON

Illahee State Park, located 3 miles northeast of Bremerton on State Route 306, consists of 75 acres of parkland offering picnic areas, hiking trails, a boat ramp, fishing, scuba diving and water-skiing.

Scenic Beach State Park consists of 88 acres, located 12 miles northwest of Bremerton at Seabeck. Visitors to the park will find picnic areas, hiking trails, fishing and scuba diving.

BRIDGEPORT

Bridgeport State Park is a 758-acre park located less than 1 mile north of Bridgeport via State Route 17. The park offers picnic areas, a boat ramp, boat rentals, water-skiing, fishing, swimming and golf.

BRINNON

Dosewallips State Park, located at Brinnon off U.S. Highway 101, is a 425-acre park offering picnic areas, hiking and bicycle trails, boating and fishing.

BURLINGTON

Bay View State Park is a 25-acre park located 7 miles west of Burlington via State Route 20. The park offers picnic areas, boating, fishing and scuba diving.

CAMANO ISLAND

Camano Island State Park, located 14 miles southwest of Stanwood on Camano Island, is a 134-acre park offering picnic areas, hiking trails, a boat ramp, fishing, swimming and scuba diving.

CASTLE ROCK

Seaquest State Park encompasses 296 acres of parkland, located 5 miles east of Castle Rock off Interstate 5, Exit 49. Visitors to the park will find areas for picnicking and fishing, as well as hiking trails.

CHEHALIS

Lewis and Clark State Park, located 12 miles southeast of Chehalis on Old State Route 99, Exit 68, is a 533-acre park offering areas for picnicking and fishing, plus hiking trails to explore.

Rainbow Falls State Park consists of 125 acres of parkland located 18 miles west of Chehalis on State Route 6. Visitors to the park will find picnic areas, hiking trails and fishing.

CHELAN

Lake Chelan State Park is a 127-acre park located 9 miles west of Chelan off U.S. Highway 97. The lake is more than 1,500 feet deep, and drops to 400 feet below sea level. Visitors to the park will find picnic areas, hiking trails, a boat ramp, fishing, swimming, scuba diving, water-skiing excursion boats and boat tours. For more information, call (509) 682-5644.

Twenty-five Mile Creek State Park, located 25 miles west of Chelan on 25-Mile Creek Road, is a 235-acre park offering picnic areas, hiking trails, a boat ramp and fishing.

CLARKSTON

Chief Timothy State Park consists of 282 acres of parkland located 8 miles west of Clarkston on U.S. Highway 12. The park offers picnic areas, hiking trails, a boat ramp, fishing, swimming, water-skiing and a visitor's center.

COULEE CITY

Sun Lakes State Park encompasses 4,024 acres of parkland located 4 miles southwest of Coulee City, off State Route 17. Here you will find picnic areas, hiking trails, horse rentals, golf, a boat ramp, boat rentals, fishing, swimming and a visitor's center. For more information, call (509) 632-5583.

COUPEVILLE

Fort Casey State Park, located 3 miles south of Coupeville off State Route 20, is a 411-acre park featuring historic forts from the late 19th century. The park offers picnic areas, hiking trails, a boat ramp, fishing, scuba diving and a visitor's center. For more information, call (360) 678-4519.

South Whidbey State Park is an 85-acre park located 10 miles south of Coupeville on Whidbey Island. The park offers picnic areas, hiking trails, fishing and scuba diving.

DAYTON

Lewis and Clark Trail State Park is a 37-acre park located 4 miles west of Dayton on U.S. Highway 12. This historic park offers picnic areas, hiking trails, fishing and winter sports.

DES MOINES

Saltwater State Park, located 2 miles south of downtown Des Moines off Marine View Drive, is a 90-acre park offering picnic areas, hiking trails, fishing, scuba diving and swimming.

EASTON

Lake Easton State Park is a 196-acre park located at Easton, off Interstate 90. Visitors to the park will find picnic areas, hiking trails, a boat ramp, fishing, swimming and winter sports such as snowmobiling.

ENUMCLAW

Kanaskat-Palmer State Park is a 297-acre park located 11 miles northeast of Enumclaw. The park offers picnic areas, hiking trails, fishing, kayaking and rafting.

Nolte State Park, located 6 miles northeast of Enumclaw off State Route 169, is a 117-acre park with picnic areas, hiking trails, a boat ramp, fishing and swimming.

GOLD BAR

Wallace Falls State Park encompasses 678 acres of parkland, located 2 miles northeast of Gold Bar off U.S. Highway 2. Visitors to the park will find areas for picnicking and fishing as well as hiking trails.

GOLDENDALE

Goldendale State Park, located 12 miles northeast of Goldendale off U.S. Highway 97, encompasses 700 acres of parkland and offers picnic areas, hiking trails, fishing, snowmobiling and a visitor's center.

Maryhill State Park, located 12 miles south of Goldendale on U.S. Highway 97, is a 98-acre park offering picnic areas, hiking trails, boating, fishing, swimming and water-skiing.

GRAND COULEE

Steamboat Rock State Park encompasses 3,523 acres of parkland, located 11 miles south of Grand Coulee on State Route 155. Visitors to the park will find picnic areas, hiking trails, a boat ramp, fishing, swimming, water-skiing and winter sports.

GRAYLAND

Grayland Beach State Park is a 411-acre park located in Grayland on State Route 105. Enjoy the hiking and bicycle trails and fishing areas.

HOODSPORT

Lake Cushman State Park, located 7 miles northwest of Hoodsport via State Route 119, offers picnic areas, hiking trails, a boat ramp, fishing, swimming and water-skiing.

ILWACO

Fort Canby State Park encompasses 1,882 acres of parkland located 3 miles southwest of Ilwaco, off U.S. Highway 101. Visitors to this historic park will find picnic areas, hiking trails, boating, fishing and a visitor's center. For more information, call (360) 642-3029.

ISSAQUAH

Lake Sammanish State Park, located 2 miles northwest of Issaquah via Interstate 90, is a 432-acre park offering picnic areas, hiking trails, a boat ramp, fishing, swimming and water-skiing.

LAKE BAY

Joemma Beach State Park consists of 170 acres of parkland located 4 miles southwest of Lake Bay on Case Inlet. Visitors to the park will find picnic areas, a boat ramp, fishing, scuba diving and water-skiing.

LEAVENWORTH

Lake Wenatchee State Park, located 22 miles north of Leavenworth off State Route 207, is a 489-acre park offering picnic areas, hiking trails, a boat ramp, boat rentals, fishing, swimming, horse rentals, skiing and snowmobiling.

LONG BRANCH

Penrose Point State Park consists of 152 acres of parkland located 3 miles north of Long Branch on State Route 302. Enjoy the picnic areas, hiking trails, a boat ramp and fishing.

LOPEZ ISLAND

Spencer Spit State Park encompasses 130 acres of parkland located on the east side of Lopez Island. Here you will enjoy hiking trails, boating, fishing and scuba diving.

LYLE

Dougs Beach State Park is a 31-acre park located 2 miles east of Lyle. The park offers windsurfing and areas for fishing and swimming.

MARYSVILLE

Wenberg State Park, located 4 miles north of Marysville via Interstate 5, then 8 miles west off State Route 531, is a 46-acre park with picnic areas, trails, a boat ramp, fishing, swimming and water-skiing.

MONTESANO

Lake Sylvia State Park, located 1 mile north of Montesano off U.S. Highway 12, Exit 104, is a 234-acre park offering picnic areas, hiking trails, a boat ramp, boat rentals, fishing and swimming. For more information, call (360) 249-5522.

MOSES LAKE

Moses Lake State Park is a 78-acre park located 5 miles west of Moses Lake off Interstate 90. Visitors will find picnic areas, a boat ramp, fishing, swimming, scuba diving and water-skiing.

Potholes Reservation State Park consists of 640 acres of parkland located 10 miles southeast of Moses Lake on State Route 17, then 14 miles west on State Route 170. The park offers picnic areas, hiking trails, a boat ramp and fishing.

MOSSYROCK

Ike Kinswa State Park, located 5 miles northwest of Mossyrock via U.S. Highway 12, is a 454-acre park offering picnic areas, hiking and bicycle trails, a boat ramp, fishing, swimming and water-skiing.

MUKILTEO

Mukilteo State Park is an 18-acre park located at Mukilteo. Visitors to the park will find picnic areas, a boat ramp, fishing and scuba diving.

OAK HARBOR

Deception Pass State Park encompasses 4,124 acres of parkland, located 9 miles west of Oak Harbor on Whidbey Island. The park offers picnic areas, hiking trails, a boat ramp, fishing, swimming, scuba diving and a visitor's center. For more information, call (360) 675-2417.

Fort Ebey State Park, located 8 miles south of Oak Harbor off State Route 20, is a 229-acre park offering picnic areas, hiking trails, scuba diving and fishing.

OCEAN CITY

Ocean City State Park is a 112-acre park located at the south edge of Ocean City, off State Route 109. The park offers hiking trails, fishing, scuba diving and a visitor's center.

OLYMPIA

Tolmie State Park, located 8 miles northeast of Olympia off Interstate 5, is a 106-acre park offering picnic areas, hiking trails, fishing, scuba diving and an underwater park.

ORCAS ISLAND

Moran State Park encompasses 4,606 acres of parkland on Orcas Island, accessible by ferry from Anacortes. The park offers picnic areas, hiking trails, a boat ramp, boat rentals, fishing and swimming.

Sucia Island State Park is a 564-acre park located 2.5 miles north of Orcas Island. The park is accessible only by boat, but it offers picnic areas, hiking trails, boating and fishing.

OLYMPIA

Millersylvania State Park encompasses 841 acres of parkland, located 10 miles south of Olympia, off Interstate 5. Visitors to the park will find picnic areas, hiking trails, boating, fishing and swimming.

OMAK

Conconully State Park consists of an 80-acre park, located 18 miles northwest of Omak, off U.S. Highway 97. Enjoy the hiking trails, a boat ramp, water-skiing, fishing, winter sports such as snowmobiling and a visitor's center.

ORONDO

Daroga State Park is a 47-acre park located 6 miles north of Orondo. Visitors to the park will find picnic areas, a ball park, tennis, hiking and bicycle trails, a boat ramp, fishing, swimming and water-skiing.

OROVILLE

Osoyoos Lake State Park, located 1 mile north of Oroville on U.S. Highway 97, is a 46-acre historic park offering picnic areas, hiking trails, a boat ramp, fishing, swimming, water-skiing and ice-skating.

PACIFIC BEACH

Pacific Beach State Park is a 9-acre park located in Pacific Beach. The park offers picnic areas, hiking trails, fishing, clamming and swimming.

PASCO

Sacajawea State Park consists of 284 acres of parkland, located 3 miles southeast of Pasco off U.S. Highway 12, at the confluence of the Snake and Columbia rivers. This historic park offers a boat ramp, fishing, swimming, water-skiing and a visitor's center. For more information, call (509) 545-2361.

PATEROS

Alta Lake State Park, located 2 miles southwest of Pateros off State Route 164, is a 177-acre park offering picnic areas, hiking trails, a boat ramp, water-skiing, scuba diving, swimming, fishing and winter sports such as snowmobiling.

POMEROY

Central Ferry State Park is a 185-acre park, located 22 miles northwest of Pomeroy on State Route 127. Enjoy the hiking trails, a boat ramp, water-skiing, fishing and swimming.

PORT ORCHARD

Manchester State Park, located 6 miles northeast of Port Orchard via Beach Drive, is a 111-acre park offering picnic areas, hiking trails, boating, fishing and scuba diving.

PORT TOWNSEND

Fort Flagler State Park, located 20 miles southeast of Port Townsend on Marrowstone Island, is a 783-acre historic park offering picnic areas, hiking and bicycle trails, a boat ramp, fishing and scuba diving. For more information, call (360) 385-1259 or 385-3701.

Fort Worden State Park is a 137-acre historic coastal fortress located 1 mile north of Port Townsend via Cherry Street. Here you will find picnic areas, hiking and bicycle trails, a boat ramp, fishing, scuba diving and a visitor's center. For more information, call (360) 385-4730.

Old Fort Townsend State Park, located 3 miles south of Port Townsend off State Route 20, is a 377-acre historic park and wildlife sanctuary that offers picnic areas, hiking trails and fishing.

POULSBO

Kitsap Memorial State Park, located 6 miles north of Poulsbo off State Route 3, is a 58-acre park offering picnic areas, hiking trails, fishing and scuba diving.

REPUBLIC

Curlew Lake State Park consists of 123 acres of parkland, located 10 miles northeast of Republic on State Route 21. The park offers picnic areas, hiking trails, a boat ramp, fishing, swimming, water-skiing and snowmobiling.

SATSOP

Schafer State Park, located 8 miles north of Satsop on the Satsop River, is a 119-acre park offering areas for picnicking and fishing, as well as hiking trails.

SEATTLE

Blake Island Marine State Park is a 473-acre park located 4 miles west of Seattle, accessible only by boat. Visitors to the park will find picnic areas, hiking trails, beach access, a boat ramp, water-skiing, scuba diving, clamming and fishing. For more information, call (206) 731-0770 for park information and (206) 443-1244 for boat departure times.

SEQUIM

Sequim Bay State Park is a 92-acre park located 7 miles southeast of Sequim, off U.S. Highway 101. Visitors to the park will find picnic areas, hiking trails, fishing and scuba diving.

SHELTON

Jarrell Cove State Park is located 15 miles northeast of Shelton off State Route 3 on Hartstene Island. This 43-acre park offers picnic areas, hiking trails, boating, fishing and scuba diving.

Potlatch State Park is a 57-acre park located north of Shelton off U.S. Highway 101. Visitors to the park will find picnic areas, hiking trails, a boat ramp, fishing, scuba diving and water-skiing.

SPOKANE

Mount Spokane State Park encompasses 13,643 acres of parkland, located 30 miles northeast of Spokane via U.S. Highway 2 and State Route 206. Visitors to the park will find picnic areas and hiking trails and winter sports such as skiing and snowmobiling.

Riverside State Park encompasses 7,469 acres of parkland, 6 miles northwest of Spokane off State Route 291. This historic park offers picnic areas, hiking trails, a boat ramp, fishing, horse rentals, winter sports and a visitor's center.

TACOMA

Dash Point State Park, located 5 miles northeast of Tacoma on State Route 509, Exit 143, is a 397-acre park offering picnic areas, hiking trails and fishing.

Kopachuck State Park consists of 109 acres of parkland, 16 miles west of Tacoma on State Route 16. Here you will find picnic areas, hiking trails, a boat ramp, fishing, scuba diving and water-skiing.

UNION

Twanoh State Park, located 5 miles east of Union on State Route 106, is a 182-acre park offering picnic areas, hiking trails, a boat ramp, fishing, swimming and water-skiing.

VANCOUVER

Beacon Rock State Park, located 35 miles east of Vancouver via State Route 14, encompasses 4,482 acres of parkland offering picnic areas, hiking and bicycle trails, a boat ramp and fishing.

Paradise Point State Park is an 88-acre park located 19 miles north of Vancouver off Interstate 5, Exit 16. Enjoy the picnic areas, hiking trails, fishing and boat ramp.

VANTAGE

Wanapum State Park, located 3 miles south of Vantage on the Columbia River, consists of 451 acres of parkland offering picnic areas, hiking trails, a boat ramp, boat rentals, fishing, swimming, water-skiing and a visitor's center.

WASHTUCNA

Lyon's Ferry State Park encompasses 1,282 acres of parkland, located 20 miles southeast of Washtucna, off State Route 261. This historic park offers picnic areas, hiking trails, a boat ramp, fishing, swimming and water-skiing.

WENATCHEE

Lincoln Rock State Park is an 80-acre park located 6 miles northeast of Wenatchee via U.S. Highway 2. Visitors will find picnic areas, hiking trails, a boat ramp, fishing, swimming, water-skiing and winter sports such as cross-country skiing.

Squilchuck State Park, located 7 miles south of Wenatchee on Squilchuck Canyon Road, is a 288-acre park offering picnic areas, hiking trails and winter sports such as snow-skiing.

Wenatchee Confluence State Park is a 91-acre park located 3 miles north of Wenatchee. Visitors will find picnic areas, hiking and bicycle trails, a boat ramp, fishing, swimming, water-skiing, tennis and ball parks.

WESTPORT

Twin Harbors State Park is a 172-acre park located 3 miles south of Westport on State Route 105. Enjoy the areas for picnicking and fishing and the hiking trails.

WHITE SALMON

Horsethief Lake State Park is a 338-acre park located 17 miles east of White Salmon off State Route 14. Visitors to the park will find Indian petroglyphs, picnic areas, hiking trails, a boat ramp and fishing.

WHITE SWAN

Fort Simcoe State Park, located 7 miles west of White Swan via State Route 220, consists of 200 acres of parkland with a historic Army post featuring a guard house and barracks. Visitors will also find picnic areas, hiking trails and a visitor's center. For more information, call (509) 874-2372.

WINSLOW

Fay Bainbridge State Park is a 17-acre park located 4 miles north of Winslow on State Route 305. Visitors to the park will find picnic areas, a boat ramp, fishing and scuba diving.

Fort Ward State Park, located 4 miles southwest of Winslow on Pleasant Beach Drive, is a 137-acre historic park offering picnic areas, hiking trails, a boat ramp, fishing, crabbing and scuba diving.

WINTHROP

Pearrygin Lake State Park encompasses 578 acres of parkland, located 5 miles northeast of Winthrop off State Route 20. You will find picnic areas, hiking trails, a boat ramp, fishing, swimming and winter sports such as snowmobiling.

YAKIMA

Yakima Sportsmen's State Park, located 1 mile east of Yakima off Interstate 82, is a 251-acre park offering picnic areas, hiking trails and fishing.

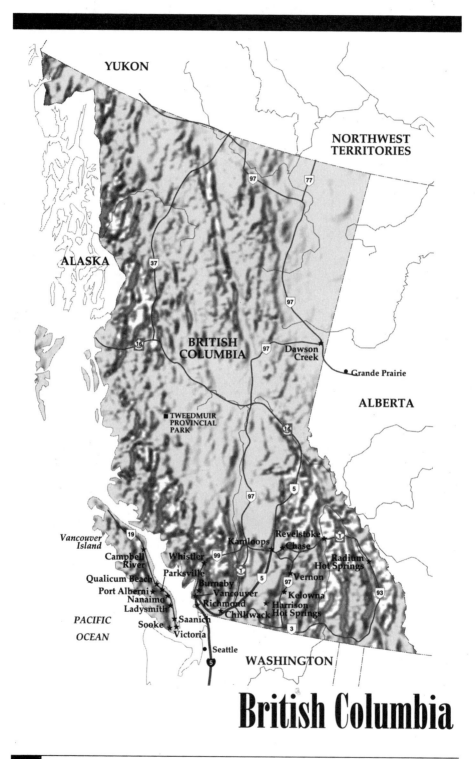

British Columbia

Pacific Northwest – British Columbia

(Please note: Room rates for accommodations in British Columbia are quoted in Canadian dollars.)

Burnaby –
Lake City Motor Inn...162

Campbell River –
Austrian Chalet – Best Western...163

Chase –
Quaaout Lodge...164

Chilliwack –
Holiday Inn – Chilliwack-Downtown...165
Travelodge...166

Dawson Creek –
Alaska Hotel...167

Harrison Hot Springs –
Harrison Hot Springs Hotel...168

Kamloops –
Courtesy Inn...169
Lac Le Jeune Resort...170
Thompson Hotel and Conference
    Centre...171
Woody Life Village Resort...172

Kelowna –
Idabel Lake Resort...173

Ladysmith –
Inn of the Sea Resort...174

Nanaimo –
Harbourview Days Inn...175

Parksville –
Tigh-Na-Mara Resort Hotel...176

Port Alberni –
Coast Hospitality Inn...177

Qualicum Beach –
Blue Willow Bed and Breakfast...178
Old Dutch Inn...179

Radium Hot Springs –
The Chalet...180

Revelstoke –
Wayside Inn – Best Western...181

Richmond –
Delta Vancouver Airport Hotel and
    Marina...182

Saanichton –
Waddling Dog – Quality Inn...183

Sooke –
French Beach Retreats and Ocean Tree
    House...184
Ocean Wilderness Inn and Spa
    Retreat...185
Sooke Harbour House...186

Vancouver –
Georgian Court Hotel...187
Holiday Inn – Vancouver Centre...188
Holiday Inn Hotel and Suites – Vancouver
    Downtown...189
Pendrell Suites...190
Renaissance Vancouver Hotel –
    Harbourside...191

Vernon –
Maria Rose Bed and Breakfast...192

Victoria –
Dashwood Manor...193
Harbour Towers Hotel...194
Ocean Pointe Resort Hotel and Spa...195
Oxford Castle Inn...196
Sonia's Bed and Breakfast by the Sea...197

Whistler –
Delta Whistler Resort...198
Edgewater Lodge...199

Lake City Motor Inn

Lake City Motor Inn
5415 Lougheed Highway
Burnaby, British Columbia V5B 2Z7
800-694-6860 • (604) 294-5331

Room Rates:	$89 – $139. AAA discount.
Pet Charges or Deposits:	$5 per day. Manager's approval required. Small pets only.
Rated: 3 Paws 🐾🐾🐾	42 guest rooms and 6 two-bedroom suites with kitchenettes, heated outdoor swimming pool and Jacuzzi, laundry facilities and coffee shop.

S et in a quiet, residential neighborhood, the family-run Lake City Motor Inn features several cedar buildings housing spacious guest accommodations and two-bedroom suites with kitchenettes. The landscaped grounds are a dog's delight, with lots of room to roam.

Located only fifteen minutes from downtown Vancouver, the inn is a great place to enjoy all the downtown attractions the city has to offer. There are theaters, great shopping, and parks for you and your dog to explore, with jogging and bicycle paths nearby.

Austrian Chalet – Best Western

Austrian Chalet – Best Western
462 South Island Highway
Campbell River, British Columbia V9W 1A5
800-667-7207 • (250) 923-4231
Website: www.vquest.com/austrian
E-mail: austrian@vquest.coms

Room Rates:	$59 – $124. AAA, AARP, AKC and ABA discounts.
Pet Charges or Deposits:	$7. Small pets only.
Rated: 3 Paws 🐾 🐾 🐾	55 guest rooms and 3 luxury suites with some efficiencies, a putting green, heated indoor swimming pool, sauna, whirlpool, exercise room, laundry facilities, restaurant and pub.

N estled along the edge of the Pacific Ocean in beautiful Campbell River is the Austrian Chalet – Best Western. The chalet provides a variety of rooms to accommodate vacationers and pets, all with panoramic ocean and mountain views.

The area offers golfing, freshwater and saltwater fishing, kayaking, whale-watching, snow-skiing and much more. Be sure to cruise the Island Highway's scenic drive to get the full beauty of the area. To relax or rejuvenate yourself, there is an indoor heated swimming pool, whirlpool, sauna and spa, plus a sun deck and exercise room so you won't miss your workout.

Quaaout Lodge

Quaaout Lodge
Little Shuswap Lake Road
P.O. Box 1215
Chase, British Columbia V0E 1M0
800-663-4303 • (250) 679-3090

Room Rates:	$79 – $160. AAA and AARP discounts.
Pet Charges or Deposits:	$5 per day.
Rated: 3 Paws 🐾 🐾 🐾	66 guest rooms and 6 suites, some with whirlpools and fireplaces, beach, heated indoor pool, sauna, whirlpool, boat dock and ramp, exercise room, playground, laundry facilities, some refrigerators, a restaurant and lounge.

L ocated on the shore of the Little Shuswap Lake, the Quaaout Lodge is like no other. Rich in tradition, the Lodge is unique in its picturesque location, its warm, friendly people and the ability to make you feel right at home. The Lodge offers a variety of accommodations, all uniquely decorated.

With 2,400 feet of sandy beach, guests can swim, canoe, fish for trout, sail, water-ski, enjoy horseback riding, whitewater rafting or simply catch the rays.

The Lodge dining room has a talented staff to provide you with delicacies that honor the native tradition of the region.

Holiday Inn – Chilliwack-Downtown

Holiday Inn – Chilliwack-Downtown
45920 First Avenue
Chilliwack, British Columbia V2P 7K1
800-520-7555 • (604) 795-4788

Room Rates:	$69 – $129. AAA and AARP discounts.
Pet Charges or Deposits:	$10 per day.
Rated: 3 Paws 🐾🐾🐾	107 guest rooms and 3 spacious suites, with panoramic views of the Fraser Valley, Coastal and Cascade Mountains, indoor waveless lap pool, Jacuzzi, sauna, fitness center, restaurant and lounge.

L ocated one hour east of Vancouver on a serene lake, with breathtaking mountain views, is the Holiday Inn – Chilliwack-Downtown. Here you will find tastefully appointed guest rooms and suites with king-sized or double beds.

Overlooking the lake is the fitness center, where guests will find the latest in fitness equipment. A workout can be followed by a soak in the Jacuzzi, a warm sauna, or a swim in the waveless lap pool.

Travelodge

Travelodge
45466 Yale Road West
Chilliwack, British Columbia V2R 1A9
800-566-2511 • (604) 792-4240

Room Rates:	$66 – $80.
Pet Charges or Deposits:	$5, plus $50 refundable deposit.
Rated: 3 Paws	82 guest rooms with mountain and countryside views, some efficiencies, heated indoor pool, whirlpool, laundry facilities and restaurant.

S et in the beautiful Fraser Valley, one hour east of Vancouver, is the Travelodge of Chilliwack. Choose from spacious guest rooms or efficiency rooms with the added convenience of an in-room refrigerator.

You and your dog will want to spend some time exploring the Fraser Valley, with its picturesque mountains, surrounding lakes and parks. You will find fishing, hiking trails, whitewater rafting, golf courses, Cultus Lake Beaches and Water Park, Harrison Hot Springs, horseback riding and, in the winter, snow-skiing. When the weather is warm, take a picnic lunch to Bridal Falls Provincial Park for a taste of the real outdoors.

Alaska Hotel

Alaska Hotel
Box 246
Dawson Creek, British Columbia V I G 4G7
(250) 782-7998

Room Rates: $25 – $45.
Pet Charges or Deposits: $5.
Rated: 3 Paws 🐾 🐾 🐾   12 guest rooms with no televisions or telephones in the rooms; a swimming pool, restaurant and cocktail lounge.

L ocated 55 paces south of the Mile Zero Post in Dawson Creek is the Alaska Hotel. Combining the spirit of Northern adventure with Old World charm, the rooms have been beautifully renovated, making your stay more like visiting a museum or stepping back in to the 1890s. The guest rooms allow you to escape from the disturbance of telephones and television and slip into the peace and privacy of days of old.

You will find plenty of activities in the area to keep you busy: horseback riding, swimming, fishing, river-boating and nature walks.

For your nightly entertainment, the Dew Drop Inn Pub features entertainment, and the world-famous Alaska Café features Peace Country Cuisine, combining the charm of a Paris café with the spirit of the adventurous north.

Harrison Hot Springs Hotel

Harrison Hot Springs Hotel
100 Esplanade Avenue
Harrison Hot Springs, British Columbia V0M 1K0
800-663-2266 • (604) 796-2244
E-mail: hhsph@uniserve.com

Room Rates:	$109 – $200, including complimentary afternoon tea. Special packages available.
Pet Charges or Deposits:	None. Reservations supervisor's approval required.
Rated: 3 Paws 🐾 🐾 🐾	306 guest rooms and 13 luxury suites, water park and playground, heated outdoor pool, indoor mineral hot springs pool, massage therapy, tennis courts, bicycle rentals, exercise and sports facilities, PGA-rated 9-hole golf course, two restaurants and a coffee bar.

L ocated in a serene lakeside setting surrounded by mountains, is the 6,000-square-foot natural mineral hot springs pools and saunas at the Harrison Hot Springs Hotel. Leave the stresses of the world behind you at this historic landmark resort.

Treat yourself to a relaxing, therapeutic massage, followed by a visit to the heated indoor pool or one of the two natural mineral hot springs pools, fed by a stream and a cascading waterfall amid an intricate rock formation. The children will love the game room, the water park and the playground. There are even supervised children's programs throughout the year. If you are still full of energy, you and your dog can stroll through the gardens, go hiking, or venture down to the lake for a little fishing. There are also tennis courts, the PGA-rated 9-hole golf course, bicycling, wind-surfing and water-skiing.

Courtesy Inn

Courtesy Inn
1773 East Trans Canada Highway
Kamloops, British Columbia V2G 3Z6
800-372-8533 • (250) 372-8533

Room Rates:	$60 – $110. AAA, AARP, AKC and ABA discounts.
Pet Charges or Deposits:	$7. No large dogs, please.
Rated: 3 Paws 🐾🐾🐾	40 guest rooms and 5 spacious suites with fully equipped kitchens, laundry facilities, indoor heated swimming pool, spa and outdoor patio.

T he Courtesy Inn is a good choice for those wishing to get the most for their travel dollars. Spacious guest rooms are professionally designed with king-sized or queen-sized beds. Fully equipped kitchens are available in the one bedroom suites.

The Inn features an indoor heated swimming pool, spa and sun deck. The location is convenient for visiting local golf courses and area ski resorts. Lac Le Jeune Lake, famous for its trout fishing, is a great escape for both you and your dog. Besides fishing, there are lots of hiking trails to explore, as well as picnic areas, boating and swimming.

Lac Le Jeune Resort

Lac Le Jeune Resort
Lac Le Jeune Road
c/o 650 Victoria Street
Kamloops, British Columbia V2C 2B4
800-561-5253 • (250) 372-2722

Room Rates:	$79 – $164.
Pet Charges or Deposits:	None. Manager's approval required.
Rated: 3 Paws 🐾 🐾 🐾	28 guest rooms and 10 fully equipped cabins, lakefront property with whirlpool, horseback riding, guided fishing tours, boating and canoeing, hiking trails, nature walks, restaurant and cocktail lounge.

L ocated south of Kamloops, perched between two lakes with breathtaking views of the mountains, is the Lac Le Jeune Resort. Known as one of the premier trout-fishing lakes in the Pacific Northwest, Lac Le Jeune Lake draws fishermen from all over the world who have come to the resort to enjoy the first-class facilities and the jumping rainbow trout. In fact, in 1993 it was host to the World Fly-Fishing Championships.

Besides the rainbow trout, there are osprey, bald eagles, loons and numerous other species of birds, as well as muskrats and beaver. For those who don't wish to fish, there are extraordinary horseback riding, hiking trails for you and your dog to explore, mountain biking, boating and swimming.

Thompson Hotel and Conference Centre

Thompson Hotel and Conference Centre
650 Victoria Street
Kamloops, British Columbia V2C 2B4
800-561-5253 • (250) 374-1999
E-mail: lejeune@mail.netshop.net

Room Rates:	$59 – $105.
Pet Charges or Deposits:	None. Manager's approval required.
Rated: 3 Paws 🐾 🐾 🐾	96 guest rooms and 3 spacious suites, indoor swimming pool and hot tub, fitness center, game room, laundry facilities, restaurant, sports bar and grill.

G entrally located in the heart of downtown Kamloops, within walking distance of art galleries, museums, parks and other area attractions, is the Thompson Hotel.

The game room, which is equipped with card tables, pool tables, Ping-Pong, fooseball and air hockey, just to name a few, is a great way to entertain children of all ages.

Whether you spend the day relaxing by the hot tub, swimming in the pool, working out in the fitness room, or taking in the local sights, you will appreciate returning to the comfort of your room. Local parks are located near the hotel where you can exercise your dog.

Woody Life Village Resort

Woody Life Village Resort
Lac Le Juene Road
c/o 650 Victoria Street
Kamloops, British Columbia V2C 2B4
800-561-5253 • (250) 374-3833

Room Rates:	$95 – $175.
Pet Charges or Deposits:	None. Manager's approval required.
Rated: 3 Paws 🐾🐾🐾	30 cabins with lake and mountain views, fully equipped kitchens, full baths, living room with sofa sleeper, indoor pool, steam sauna, whirlpool, exercise and weight room and restaurant.

L ocated at beautiful Lac Le Jeune Lake, this resort offers deluxe log cabins with large decks for enjoying the views of the lake and mountains. These individual one-bedroom units have a separate living area with a sofa sleeper, full bath and a fully equipped kitchen, although the chef will be glad to prepare your meals for you.

Built in 1990, the resort sits next to a pond and a bird sanctuary, where you will find wildflowers, marmots, squirrels, loons and incredible bird life. There is a wide range of indoor and outdoor activities for you to enjoy here. The main lodge also has a movie theater, game room, indoor pool, whirlpool, steam sauna and a fully equipped exercise room.

Idabel Lake Resort

Idabel Lake Resort
12000 Highway 33E, No. 4
Kelowna, British Columbia V1P 1K4
(250) 765-9511

Room Rates:	$75 – $175.
Pet Charges or Deposits:	None.
Rated: 4 Paws	8 private cottages and 5 condo suites, some with private hot tubs. Boat dock, tennis court, barbecue area and playground.

S et on a tranquil mountain lake, only minutes from Kelowna and Big White Mountain, is Idabel Lake Resort. This unique, family-oriented resort offers guests their choice of deluxe accommodations, with city services and the tranquillity of a wilderness setting.

There are eight country cottages with fully equipped kitchens, living and dining rooms, some with private hot tubs and small balconies overlooking the lake, with picturesque views of Little White Mountain in the distance. Situated below the cottages are five condos with two or three bedrooms each, overlooking the lake.

The area is abundantly populated with wildlife: deer, elk, beavers, otters and even a family of loons living on the lake. It's not uncommon to see moose grazing by the water's edge in the evening. Located only three miles from the resort are historic Kettle Valley and Myra Canyon, where you will find spectacular wooden trestle bridges, old tunnels and breathtaking views of the valley.

Inn of the Sea Resort

Inn of the Sea Resort
3600 Yellow Point Road
R.R. 3
Ladysmith, British Columbia V0R 2E0
800-548-0310 • (250) 245-1011
Web Site: www.innofthesea.com
E-mail: info@innofthesea.com

Room Rates: $60 – $165.
Pet Charges or Deposits: $10 per week.
Rated: 4 Paws 🐾 🐾 🐾 🐾 600 guest rooms and suites with balconies or sun decks, kitchen facilities, wood-burning fireplaces, pool, hot tub and tennis court.

S it back and watch the eagles glide over the top of the ancient forest or watch the sun rise over Galiano Island. Enjoy the oceanside hot tub and heated outdoor pool, or just unwind in one of the suites with a wood-burning fireplace. The Inn of the Sea offers a unique combination of facilities and the warm hospitality of a country setting.

Guest rooms and suites are tastefully appointed for relaxing comfort. One-or two-bedroom suites have spacious living rooms with fireplaces, separate dining areas and modern, fully equipped kitchens. All units have full baths, individual balconies and private entrances.

Harbourview Days Inn

Harbourview Days Inn
809 Island Highway South
Nanaimo, British Columbia V9R 5K1
800-DAYS-INN • (250) 754-8171

Room Rates:	$59 – $85.
Pet Charges or Deposits:	$7 per stay.
Rated: 3 Paws 🐾 🐾 🐾	79 guest rooms, some with kitchenettes, views of the bay, indoor swimming pool, whirlpool, laundry facilities and family-style restaurant.

L ocated in picturesque Nanaimo, known as the "Hub City" because of its central location, is the Harbourview Days Inn, offering easy access to British Columbia ferries from Horseshoe Bay, Tsawwassen terminals and the scenic Island Highway.

Many of the Inn's comfortable guest rooms offer kitchenettes for those who wish to do a little light cooking, and a family-style restaurant for those who don't, as well as views of the bay, the offshore islands and the beautiful mountains.

The inn's spacious, landscaped grounds are the perfect place for you and your dog to take a morning stroll before you head out for a day of adventure. Since Nanaimo is considered "the sun porch of Canada," it offers visitors wonderful recreation opportunities. You will find hiking trails to explore, swimming areas, sport fishing, scuba diving, picnic areas with exotic trees to shade you, plus marine wildlife tours to view sea lions and graceful bald eagles.

Tigh-Na-Mara Resort Hotel

Tigh-Na-Mara Resort Hotel
1095 East Island Highway
Parksville, British Columbia V9P 2E5
800-663-7373 • (250) 248-2072
Web Site: www.island.net/~tnm
E-mail: tnm@island.net

Room Rates:	$74 – $189. AAA discount.
Pet Charges or Deposits:	None.
Rated: 3 Paws 🐾 🐾 🐾	56 guest rooms and 86 spacious suites, some efficiencies and kitchens, fireplaces, beach, heated indoor pool, whirlpool, tennis court, exercise room, playground, laundry facilities and restaurant.

Sheltered among tall arbutus and Douglas fir trees, next to miles of sandy beaches, all of the units are constructed of logs and have forest or ocean views from every window. The cottage, lodge and condo units have stone fireplaces and private Jacuzzis.

Tigh-Na-Mara is at the center of a recreation paradise. There are literally hundreds of sights to see, places to go, shops to browse, things to do and games to play. Thanks to the mild climate, you can golf, fish and hike year-round. There are wild rivers and serene lakes, festivals and rodeos, craft shops and museums.

The resort has a wonderful indoor pool, an exercise room, a steam room and a hot tub. There are also outdoor barbecues, trampolines, watercraft rentals and tennis courts for guests to enjoy.

Coast Hospitality Inn

Coast Hospitality Inn
3835 Redford Street
Port Alberni, British Columbia V9Y 3S2
800-663-1144 • (250) 723-8111

Room Rates:	$120 – $130. AAA discount.
Pet Charges or Deposits:	None. Sorry, no cats.
Rated: 3 Paws 🐾🐾🐾	50 guest rooms, restaurant and cocktail lounge.

 t the Coast Hospitality Inn you will find homey, comfortable accommodations set in breathtaking, natural surroundings.

The city of Port Alberni is a deep-water port, offering world-class fishing and scenic cruises. There are also unique shops, charming waterfront markets, art galleries and many natural wonders to explore. The area is surrounded by mountains, lakes and forests, so there are plenty of opportunities for you and your dog to enjoy the outdoors. In the winter, nearby Mount Arrowsmith is popular with alpine and cross-country skiers.

Blue Willow Bed and Breakfast

Blue Willow Bed and Breakfast
524 Quatna Road
Qualicum Beach, British Columbia V9K 1B4
(250) 752-9052
Web Site: www.bbcanada.com/550.html
E-mail: bwillow@qb.island.net

Room Rates:	$70 - $100, including full breakfast.
Pet Charges or Deposits:	$10 per day. One night's rate refundable deposit.
Rated: 3 Paws 🐾 🐾 🐾	2 rooms and 1 suite with dog runs and exercise area. Close to civic trails, Powerhouse Trail, Powerline Trail and ocean beaches.

Blue Willow Bed and Breakfast offers you comfort, quiet and relaxation in a beautiful cottage garden setting. Leaded glass windows and beamed ceilings are features of this lovely Tudor-style home, which is set amid a profusion of flowers, shrubs and tall evergreen trees.

Delightfully appointed guest rooms offer a choice of king-sized, queen-sized or twin beds with private bath. There is also a charming suite of rooms separate from the main house.

An elegant breakfast is served on the blue and white china from which the bed and breakfast takes its name. The changing menu, which is bountiful, always includes home baking and either continental or English breakfast fare.

A long-established and respected bed and breakfast, Blue Willow is located 500 meters from the beach on the Strait of Georgia at Qualicum Beach and 45 kilometers northwest of the Nanaimo ferry terminal on Vancouver Island.

Old Dutch Inn

Old Dutch Inn
2690 Island Highway West
Qualicum Beach, British Columbia V9K 1G8
800-661-0199 • (250) 752-6914

Room Rates: $60 – $116. Off-season and holiday packages available.
Pet Charges or Deposits: $10 per day.
Rated: 3 Paws 🐾 🐾 🐾   34 guest rooms and 1 suite, heated indoor pool, sauna and spa, restaurant and cocktail lounge.

onveniently located directly across the street from the beach is the Old Dutch Inn. The oceanview rooms have comfortable patios where you can relax and watch gorgeous sunsets.

The indoor heated swimming pool, whirlpool and sauna offer a welcome respite after a long day of traveling, sightseeing, playing golf on one of the local courses, taking a charter fishing trip, or, in the winter, taking advantage of the nearby snow-skiing.

The inn's dining room overlooks picturesque Qualicum Beach and is a "must try" for their world-famous cakes.

The Chalet

The Chalet
5063 Madsen Road
Radium Hot Springs, British Columbia V0A 1M0
(250) 347-9305

Room Rates:	$85 – $125, including continental breakfast.
Pet Charges or Deposits:	$10 per day. Manager's approval required. Sorry, no cats.
Rated: 4 Paws 🐾🐾🐾🐾	17 studio suites with efficiency kitchens, panoramic mountain and valley views, decks, sauna, Jacuzzi, game area, exercise room, barbecue area, hiking and jogging trails; located near Kootenay National Park.

L ocated above Radium Hot Springs, The Chalet offers studio suites with spectacular, panoramic views of the Columbia Valley. Each suite is equipped with a microwave, refrigerator and sink, making it an excellent choice for an extended stay or a weekend getaway.

Bordering the British Columbia Rockies, The Chalet provides convenient access to a virtual playground that allows for a wide range of recreational activities.

Only steps from your door you will find cross-country skiing, or enjoy downhill skiing at Kimberley's, only an hour away. Fishermen will find a true paradise in the Vermilion, Simpson and Kootenay rivers. The entire family can saddle up for a leisurely afternoon ride on trails winding through the mountainous terrain. Swimming is available year-round in the warm waters of both Radium and Fairmount Hot Springs, and Lake Windermere offers warm waters for summer swimming.

Wayside Inn – Best Western

Wayside Inn – Best Western
1901 Laforme Boulevard
P.O. Box 59
Revelstoke, British Columbia V0E 2S0
800-528-1234 • (250) 837-6161

Room Rates:	$79 – $139. AAA and AARP discounts.
Pet Charges or Deposits:	None.
Rated: 3 Paws 🐾 🐾 🐾	88 guest rooms, some with refrigerators; heated indoor swimming pool, sauna, whirlpool, restaurant and cocktail lounge.

L ocated near Glacier National Park, in the shadows of Mount Revelstoke, is the Wayside Inn – Best Western. Here you will find spacious, air-conditioned accommodations that include comfortable queen-sized beds and a quiet location.

Be sure to visit Mount Revelstoke National Park, a great place to delight in picnics and fishing and to experience the magnificent mountains. You will also want to spend some time at Glacier National Park, where the rugged terrain offers hiking trails for you and your dog to explore.

Delta Vancouver Airport Hotel and Marina

Delta Vancouver Airport Hotel and Marina
3500 Cessna Drive
Richmond, British Columbia V7B 1C7
800-268-1133 • (604) 278-1241

Room Rates:	$159 – $300. AAA discount.
Pet Charges or Deposits:	None.
Rated: 3 Paws 🐾🐾🐾	412 guest rooms and 3 luxury suites with mini-bars, some whirlpool tubs, 8 riverfront acres, outdoor swimming pool, poolside patio and bar service, jogging trails, complimentary passes for nearby recreation facilities, workout studio, boat dock and marina, room service, restaurants and cocktail lounge.

S et on eight scenic acres along the Fraser River is the Delta Vancouver Airport Hotel and Marina. This full-service hotel offers guests spacious rooms and suites, many with spectacular views of the river.

A workout studio is located on the top floor, overlooking the scenic West Coast Mountains, as is the outdoor pool with poolside patio and bar service. A jogging trail along the riverfront is a great place to exercise your dog.

Waddling Dog — Quality Inn

Waddling Dog — Quality Inn
2476 Mt. Newton Crossroad
Saanichton, British Columbia V8M 2B8
800-567-8466 • (250) 652-1146

Room Rates:	$69 – $135, including deluxe continental breakfast. AAA, AARP, AKC and ABA discounts.
Pet Charges or Deposits:	$5 per day.
Rated: 3 Paws 🐾 🐾 🐾	30 guest rooms, restaurant and cocktail lounge.

T he site where the 30-room Waddling Dog – Quality Inn now stands has an interesting history. Originally a small farm, the land was purchased and the abandoned farmhouse was donated and removed from the site. An architect was brought in from Scotland to design an "Old English-style pub," and five years later the Waddling Dog, a restaurant, pub and hotel, was born. The unusual name of the inn refers to the resident that moved in and took care of the building, a beloved basset hound named John. Today John's successor, John II, presides over the property.

Guests will find comfortable guest rooms furnished with English antiques, an English pub and Basil's, a family-style restaurant.

The Saanich Peninsula is located only fifteen minutes from Victoria and it offers hiking trails, beaches, horseback riding, fishing and boating.

French Beach Retreats and Ocean Tree House

French Beach Retreats and Ocean Tree House
983 Seaside Drive
Mailing Address: 969 Seaside Drive
Sooke, British Columbia V0S 1N0
(250) 646-2154
Web Site: www.sookenet.com
E-mail: fbr@islandnet.com

Room Rates:	$165 – $275, including continental breakfast.
Pet Charges or Deposits:	$10 per day. Credit card as deposit.
Rated: 4 Paws 🐾🐾🐾🐾	2- or 3-bedroom, 2 bath vacation homes for up to 8 guests, located near the beach and national park, with ocean-view decks, wood-burning fireplaces, fully equipped kitchens, laundry facilities and Jacuzzi tubs.

T ake your pick: choose the Ocean Treehouse, a peaceful, secluded, cozy cottage in the woods, or The Retreat, if exclusive use of an 1,800-square-foot oceanfront cedar home sounds more intriguing. Both reside on more than three acres of old-growth woods with trails leading to rocky, secluded shores.

The octagonal Treehouse is small but inviting, surrounded by windows, with hardwood floors and Turkish rugs. A queen-sized bed, covered with fluffy down comforters, bookshelves crammed with books and knickknacks and fresh fruit and wine greet you upon arrival. A compact refrigerator holds the supplies for your continental breakfast.

The Retreat, a contemporary coastal property, accommodates up to eight guests. This fully equipped three-bedroom home offers a Jacuzzi tub for two, a full kitchen with all the breakfast fixings included and a double-sided woodh-burning fireplace to keep you cozy and warm.

Since both accommodations are within minutes of the park and beach, it is a wonderful choice for both you and your pet.

Ocean Wilderness Inn and Spa Retreat

Ocean Wilderness Inn and Spa Retreat
109 West Coast Road
Sooke, British Columbia V0S 1N0
800-323-2116 • (250) 646-2116
Web Site: www.sookenet.com/ocean
E-mail: ocean@sookenet.com

Room Rates:	$85 – $175, including full breakfast. AAA, AARP, AKC and ABA discounts.
Pet Charges or Deposits:	$10 per day.
Rated: 4 Paws 🐾🐾🐾🐾	9 guest rooms set on 5 acres, all furnished in antiques, with landscaped gardens, private balconies and patios, and full spa facilities.

Set on five acres of old-growth rain forest on the picturesque southern coast of Vancouver Island is the Ocean Wilderness Inn and Spa Retreat, where you will revel in the natural beauty of the mountains and ocean. This relaxing retreat will impress you with its hospitality and attention to detail. Each beautifully appointed guest room is furnished with lovely antiques, featuring a king- or queen-sized canopy bed with down comforter, private bath, some with soaker tubs for two, private entrance, terry robes, mini-refrigerator, ocean and mountain views, private balcony or patio.

Start your day with a tempting breakfast of freshly baked cinnamon rolls, biscuits, homemade jellies and jams and farm-fresh eggs.

There are beautifully landscaped gardens, private beaches and acres of rain forest for you and your dog to explore. Take advantage of the full spa facilities to rejuvenate yourself with an herbal wrap, tai chi meditation, or a relaxing massage.

Sooke Harbour House

Sooke Harbour House
1528 Whiffen Spit Road
Sooke, British Columbia V0S 1N0
(250) 642-3421
Web Site: www.sookenet.com/sooke/shh
E-mail: shh@islandnet.com

Room Rates:	$175 – $350, including full breakfast. AAA discount.
Pet Charges or Deposits:	$20 per day. One night's deposit required; refundable if cancellation is prior to 15 days.
Rated: 5 Paws 🐾🐾🐾🐾🐾	10 rooms and 18 suites, each room individually decorated, with fireplaces, private balconies or decks, some with indoor Jacuzzis or outdoor hot tubs, with garden, ocean or harbor views and a restaurant.

S ooke Harbour House is perched on a bluff overlooking the Sooke Inlet, offering sweeping views of the Strait of Juan de Fuca and Washington's Olympic Mountains.

Innkeepers Fredrica and Sinclair Philip have created a wonderfully romantic little white inn by the sea, surrounded by more than 400 varieties of herbs, flowers, berries and fruit trees. Under the spell of Sooke's masterful chefs, the land and sea gardens blend to create an award-winning cuisine.

Every room is filled with antique furniture, handsewn quilts and many original artworks. All the guest rooms have ocean views, a balcony or terrace, private baths and fireplaces.

Georgian Court Hotel

Georgian Court Hotel
773 Beatty Street
Vancouver, British Columbia V6B 2M4
800-663-1155 • (604) 682-5555

Room Rates:	$110 – $250.
Pet Charges or Deposits:	$20 per stay. Small pets only.
Rated: 4 Paws 🐾🐾🐾🐾	162 guest rooms and 18 executive suites, with mini bars, health club facilities, whirlpool and sauna, restaurants and cocktail lounge.

When looking for a European-style hotel with gracious surroundings and impeccable service, The Georgian Court Hotel is an excellent choice.

Conveniently located in downtown Vancouver, this restful retreat offers spaciously appointed guest rooms and suites with hand-crafted furnishings and rich decor.

The excellent reputation of this hotel is further enhanced by their superb, award-winning dining establishments. If a fitness routine is important, the fully equipped exercise room with whirlpool and sauna will provide an invigorating workout.

Holiday Inn – Vancouver Centre

Holiday Inn – Vancouver Centre
711 West Broadway Avenue
Vancouver, British Columbia V5Z 3Y2
800-HOLIDAY • (604) 879-0511

Room Rates:	$159 – $229. AAA discount.
Pet Charges or Deposits:	None. Pets up to 40 lbs.
Rated: 3 Paws 🐾🐾🐾	194 guest rooms and 2 luxury suites, decks with water and mountain views, indoor heated swimming pool, sauna, large outdoor patio, bistro and lounge.

 ocated across from False Creek, the hotel offers some of Vancouver's most spectacular mountain and water views. The Holiday Inn's central location means you are only minutes from all the downtown attractions.

For a light snack or casual dining, the Stage Bistro and Lounge offers a fresh and imaginative menu, combining Mediterranean and West Coast flavors. It is a great place to catch your favorite sporting events. The Great King Seafood Restaurant offers a menu with seafood selections. If Lady Luck is on your side, stop by the Great Canadian Casino located within the hotel complex.

Holiday Inn Hotel and Suites – Vancouver Downtown

Holiday Inn Hotel and Suites – Vancouver Downtown
1110 Howe Street
Vancouver, British Columbia V6Z 1R2
800-663-9151 • (604) 684-2151

Room Rates:	$149 – $399. AAA, AARP, AKC and ABA discounts.
Pet Charges or Deposits:	None.
Rated: 3 Paws 🐾🐾🐾	201 guest rooms and 44 deluxe suites, some efficiencies with mini-bars, indoor heated swimming pool, saunas, exercise room, restaurant and cocktail lounge.

C onveniently located in the heart of Vancouver's central business district, the Holiday Inn Hotel and Suites offers well-appointed guest rooms and suites. If you wish to pamper yourself, there are one- and two-bedroom deluxe suites with European-style furnishings and mini-kitchens.

The hotel's multi-gym facility is available for your workout before you relax in the indoor swimming pool. There is even a Kids' Activity Centre to keep the youngsters entertained. For your four-legged family members, there is a delightful park nearby.

Pendrell Suites

Pendrell Suites
1419 Pendrell Street, No. 2
Vancouver, British Columbia V6G 1S3
888-250-7211 • (604) 685-0715
Web Site: www.pendrellsuites.com
E-mail: rosemary@pendrellsuites.com

Room Rates:	$99 – $200. Monthly rates available. AAA, AARP, AKC and ABA discounts.
Pet Charges or Deposits:	Call for charges and deposits. Manager's approval required.
Rated: 4 Paws 🐾 🐾 🐾 🐾	6 spacious two- and three-bedroom suites, full baths, hardwood floors, antique furnishings, full kitchens and dining areas, fireplaces, laundry facilities and shopping service, lovely garden with barbecue and meditation pond.

 njoy a first-class stay in one of the six exclusive "homes" while in Vancouver. There are only two grand suites per floor in this brick heritage building, which was built in 1910 and refurbished completely in 1996.

Located in a quiet residential area, suites range from 1,200 to 1,500 square feet, offering two or three bedrooms with two full baths, beautiful hardwood floors, charming antique furnishings, a fully equipped kitchen and dining area and private entrance. All the suites offer maid service and the maid will gladly prepare your breakfast or other meals for you. Pre-stocking and shopping services are an option, including ethnic and organic foods. Pendrell Suites offers a full laundry facility: either do it yourself or they will do it for you.

Take time to enjoy the meditation garden with its pond of fish and trickling water or revitalize with a walk on the seawall.

Renaissance Vancouver Hotel – Harbourside

Renaissance Vancouver Hotel – Harbourside
1133 West Hastings Street
Vancouver, British Columbia V6E 3T3
800-HOTELS-1 • (604) 689-9211

Room Rates: $167 – $380. AARP discount.
Pet Charges or Deposits: $100 refundable deposit. Manager's approval required.
Rated: 4 Paws 🐾🐾🐾🐾 439 guest rooms and 18 suites, honor bars, pool, sun deck, sauna, exercise room, revolving rooftop restaurant and cocktail lounge.

T he Renaissance Vancouver Hotel – Harbourside is a contemporary hotel offering deluxe guest rooms and spacious, individually decorated suites with panoramic harbour, city or mountain views and the variety of personal services you expect to find in a fine hotel.

To help you maintain your workout routine, the hotel's fitness center is equipped with state-of-the-art equipment, as well as an indoor swimming pool and sauna. For outdoor sports, there is a scenic jogging trail that winds through nearby Stanley Park.

The hotel adjoins the downtown financial district and is just a short walk from the popular Robson Street and Pacific Centre shopping areas. Vancouver's famous Stanley Park, Gastown and the city's many arts and cultural attractions are also nearby.

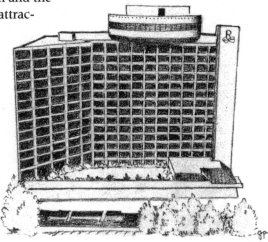

Maria Rose Bed and Breakfast

Maria Rose Bed and Breakfast
8083 Aspen Road
Vernon, British Columbia V1B 3M9
(250) 549-4773

Room Rates:	$40 – $125, including full breakfast.
Pet Charges or Deposits:	$5, plus credit card as refundable deposit.
Rated: 3 Paws 🐾 🐾 🐾	4 guest rooms with private entrances.

 ituated on a mountainside with scenic panoramic views of both Kalamalka Lake and Okanagan Lake, surrounded by the Okanagan Valley, is The Maria Rose Bed and Breakfast.

All rooms are tastefully decorated with elegant furnishings, each reflecting its own character. A scrumptious full breakfast is served in a special guest room in the main house.

Set on seven peaceful, tree-studded, secluded acres, you will enjoy privacy and comfort in this year-round retreat. At the same time, you are only a short distance from both Ellison Provincial Park and Silver Star Provincial Park, where you and your dog are welcome to explore the hiking trails.

Dashwood Manor

Dashwood Manor
One Cook Street
Victoria, British Columbia V8V 3W6
800-667-5517 • (250) 385-5517
Web Site: www.dashwoodmanor.com
E-mail: reservations@dashwoodmanor.com

Room Rates:	$125 – $285, including full breakfast. AAA, AARP, AKC and ABA discounts. Packages available.
Pet Charges or Deposits:	Call for deposit requirements.
Rated: 4 Paws 🐾🐾🐾🐾	15 suites with private baths, kitchenettes, views, private entrances and balconies.

P erched on the edge of Beacon Hill Park, overlooking the Staits of Juan de Fuca, is the Dashwood Seaside Manor Bed and Breakfast Inn. This gracious 1912 Edwardian Tudor Revival-style manor has been lovingly restored to offer guests fifteen elegant suites.

Each suite is like your own private home, complete with fully stocked kitchens, private bathrooms, some with Jacuzzis, and breathtaking views of the Inn's charming garden, the Olympic Mountains or the Staits of Juan de Fuca.

The grand main-floor suites have fireplaces, stained glass and chandeliers and are decorated with an Edwardian theme. Second-floor suites, referred to as bachelor suites, have been lovingly restored as well, but offer the additional luxury of Jacuzzis. Finally, the third-floor suites are intimate getaways with private balconies, grand bathrooms, lots of little extras and some of the best views.

The 183-acre Beacon Hill Park is located next to the Inn, and you and your pet will enjoy the park's garden, small lakes and lawns that slope all the way to the sea.

Harbour Towers Hotel

Harbour Towers Hotel
345 Quebec Street
Victoria, British Columbia V8V 1W4
800-663-5896 • (250) 385-2405

Room Rates:	$109 – $249.
Pet Charges or Deposits:	None. Small pets only.
Rated: 3 Paws 🐾 🐾 🐾	185 guest rooms and 71 suites overlooking the harbour, some efficiencies, heated indoor swimming pool, sauna, whirlpool, fitness center, restaurant and cocktail lounge.

R ight near the pulse of the city, with spectacular views of the Inner Harbour and the Straits of Juan de Fuca, is the Harbour Towers Hotel. The spacious guest rooms and suites have breathtaking views of Victoria, many with in-room Jacuzzis and wood-burning fireplaces.

Pamper yourself with a day in the esthetics studio, or soak up some sun on your own private balcony. The well-appointed fitness center and the walking/jogging path along the ocean will help you maintain your daily work-out. With the mild winters and pleasant summers of the area, you will find year-round outdoor activities, such as golf, boating, fishing and whale-watching. Of course there are plenty of local attractions, shopping areas, antique shops and fine restaurants to wile away your day.

Ocean Pointe Resort Hotel and Spa

Ocean Pointe Resort Hotel and Spa
45 Songhees Road
Victoria, British Columbia V9A 6T3
800-667-4677 • (250) 360-2999
Web Site: www.oprhotel.com
E-mail: ocean_pointe@pine.com

Room Rates:	$89 – $725. AAA, AARP, AKC and ABA discounts.
Pet Charges or Deposits:	$75 per stay. Manager's approval required. Small pets only.
Rated: 4 Paws 🐾🐾🐾🐾	250 guest rooms, 34 suites, all with honor bars, views of city or mountains, some kitchens, 2 lighted tennis courts, racquetball court, indoor heated swimming pool, sauna, whirlpool, full European spa and fitness center, restaurants and cocktail lounge.

P oised along the shore of Victoria's inner harbour is the Ocean Pointe Resort Hotel and Spa. This full-service resort hotel offers well-appointed accommodations and traditional European hospitality, with West Coast flair, plus some of the most spectacular views of the harbour in the city.

To relax and rejuvenate your body and soul, the hotel spa with has aromatherapy soaks, hydrotherapy baths, massages, facials or micronized algae body wraps. To tone and stretch your muscles, the hotel's fitness center offers superb equipment and a fitness trainer to coach you. Enjoy a game of tennis, racquetball or squash, swim a few laps in the indoor heated swimming pool, or take a sauna.

Oxford Castle Inn

Oxford Castle Inn
133 Gorge Road East
Victoria, British Columbia V0P 1G0
800-661-0322 • (250) 388-6431

Room Rates:	$68 – $128.
Pet Charges or Deposits:	$10 per day. Call for deposits. Manager's approval required. Small dogs only. Sorry, no cats.
Rated: 3 Paws 🐾 🐾 🐾	3 guest rooms and 55 spacious suites with full kitchens and separate living areas, elevator, laundry facilities, heated swimming pool, sauna and Jacuzzi.

L ocated near the Gorge waterway, about one mile from downtown Victoria, this castle-style inn, complete with turret and spiral staircase, offers guests spacious one-bedroom suites, including a fully equipped kitchens, private bedrooms and separate living rooms. These homey suites are so complete you won't even have to bring an alarm clock.

For your recreational pleasure, the Inn has a beautiful indoor heated swimming pool, a wonderful redwood sauna and a Jacuzzi to relax those tired muscles. If golf is your game, there are several courses only minutes away.

Sonia's Bed and Breakfast by the Sea

Sonia's Bed and Breakfast by the Sea
175 Bushby Street
Victoria, British Columbia V8S 1B5
800-667-4489 • (250) 385-2700

Room Rates:	$82 – $178, including full breakfast.
Pet Charges or Deposits:	None. Manager's approval required.
Rated: 3 Paws	3 guest rooms and 1 suite.

L ocated in a charming residential area of Victoria, near the scenic Inner Harbour and the shores of the Straits of Juan de Fuca, is Sonia's Bed and Breakfast by the Sea.

You will find three private guest rooms: the Queen's Room, the Captain's Room and the Oak Room, all with private baths and king- or queen-sized beds. The Penthouse Suite has more than 1,100-square-feet of living space, complete with a private sitting room and a large sun deck overlooking the ocean. The comfortable, sunny common room and landscaped yard are for you to enjoy.

Known for exquisite breakfasts, you will feast on Belgian waffles or French toast with fresh, home-grown raspberries and a varied assortment of home-made preserves.

You and your dog can explore Ebert Park and Beacon Hill Park, which are located nearby.

Delta Whistler Resort

Delta Whistler Resort
4050 Whistler Way
Whistler, British Columbia V0N 1B4
800-515-4050 • (604) 932-1982

Room Rates: $165 – $235. AAA discount.
Pet Charges or Deposits: None.
Rated: 5 Paws 🐾🐾🐾🐾🐾 268 guest rooms and 24 suites, many rooms with fireplaces, balconies, kitchens, fully equipped spa, all-weather tennis club, exercise facilities, heated outdoor swimming pool, indoor and outdoor Jacuzzis, steam room, massage and shiatsu therapy, restaurant and bar.

T his Four Diamond property is the only full-service resort hotel located at the base of both Whistler and Blackcomb Mountain gondolas. Steps from alpine skiing in North America's No. 1 rated ski resort, four championship golf courses, mountain biking, and an endless variety of all-season activities await you.

Many of the spacious accommodations include a cozy fireplace, a kitchen, and a balcony with a spectacular view of the mountains.

The fully equipped Mountain Spa and Tennis Club includes two all-weather tennis courts, exercise facilities, a heated outdoor swimming pool, both indoor and outdoor Jacuzzis, a steam room, massage and shiatsu therapy.

Edgewater Lodge

Edgewater Lodge
8841 Highway 99
Box 369
Whistler, British Columbia V0N 1B0
(604) 932-0688
Web Site: www.whistler.net/resort/edgewater
E-mail: jays@whistler.net

Room Rates: $105 – $185, including continental breakfast. AAA discount.
Pet Charges or Deposits: None.
Rated: 5 Paws 🐾🐾🐾🐾🐾 12 guest rooms, Jacuzzi, hot tub, horses, kayaks, canoes, restaurant.

E dgewater Lodge is a stunning lakeside retreat on 45 acres of beautiful, private forested land north of Whistler Village, bordering on the River of Golden Dreams. All rooms are a stone's throw from the water's edge, offering stunning views of Green Lake and Edge, Blackcomb and Whistler Mountains.

The dining room has become famous for dinner. Included in your fare are fresh fruits, homemade cereals, yogurt, hot croissants, pastries, freshly squeezed juice and as much of the great coffee as you want. The chef prepares beautiful meals, five evenings a week in an incomparable setting.

At Edgewater Lodge all you can hear are the birds singing and the water lapping at the lakeshore, adjacent your bedroom window.

WHERE TO TAKE YOUR PETS IN
BRITISH COLUMBIA

Please note: *Pets must be on a leash at all times and may be restricted to certain areas. For directions, use fees, pet charges and general information, contact the numbers listed below.*

(A hectare is equal to 2.471 acres of land.)

National Parks General Information

Environment, Lands and Parks
10334 - 152A Street
Surrey, British Columbia, Canada V3R 7P8
800-665-7027

National Parks

FIELD

Yoho National Park consists of 1,313 square kilometers of parkland, located west of the Great Divide and Banff National Park. Visitors to the park will find picnic areas, hiking and bicycling trails, boating, boat and horse rentals, fishing, winter sports and a visitor's center. For more information, call **(604) 343-6783.**

RADIUM HOT SPRINGS

Kootenay National Parks encompasses 1,406 square kilometers of parkland straddling Banff-Windermere Highway 93 and follows the Vermilion and Kootenay river valleys. It is great place to enjoy the picnic areas, hiking and bicycling trails, boating, fishing, swimming, winter sports and visitor's center. For more information, call **(604) 347-9615.**

REVELSTOKE

Glacier National Park has 1,350 square kilometers, or 521 square miles of park encompassing portions of the rugged Columbia Ranges. You will find picnic areas, hiking trails, fishing, winter sports and a visitor's center. For more information, call **(604) 837-7500.**

Mount Revelstoke National Park consists of 260 square kilometers of parkland flanked on the east by the Purcell Mountains and on the west by the Monashee Range. The park offers picnic areas, hiking trails, fishing and winter sports. For more information, call **(604) 937-7500.**

VANCOUVER ISLAND

Pacific Rim National Park is 510 square kilometers of parkland divided into three sections, on the west coast of Vancouver Island: Long Beach between Ucluelet and Tofino, Broken Island Group, which is a cluster of islands in Barkley Sound, and the West Coast trail between Banfield and Port Renfrew. Enjoy picnic areas, hiking trails, boating, fishing, swimming and the visitor's center. For more information, call (604) 726-7721.

Provincinal Parks General Information

British Columbia Parks
800 Johnson Street
Victoria, British Columbia,
Canada V8V 1X4
387-5002 – information

Environment, Lands and Parks
10334 - 152A Street
Surrey, British Columbia,
Canada V3R 7P8
800-665-7027 – information

Provincinal Parks

70-MILE HOUSE

Green Lake Provincial Park, located 16 kilometers east of Highway 97 at 70-Mile House, is a 347-hectare park offering picnic areas, a boat ramp, fishing and swimming.

93-MILE HOUSE

Bridge Lake Provincial Park is a 6-hectare park located 51 miles east of 93-Mile House off Highway 24. The park offers picnic areas, hiking trails, a boat ramp, fishing and swimming.

100-MILE HOUSE

Canim Beach Provincial Park, located 43 kilometers east of 100-Mile House off Highway 97, is a 6-hectare park offering picnic areas, boating, fishing and swimming.

150-MILE HOUSE

Horsefly Lake Provincial Park encompasses 148 hectares of parkland and is located 68 kilometers east of 150-Mile House, off Highway 97. You will find picnic areas, a boat ramp, fishing and swimming.

BURNS LAKE

Ethel F. Wilson Memorial Provincial Park is a 29-hectare park located 24 kilometers north of Highway 16 at Burns Lake. Enjoy picnic areas, hiking trails, a boat ramp, fishing and swimming.

Pendleton Bay Provincial Park consists of 8 hectares of parkland, 35 kilometers north of Burns Lake off Highway 16. Visitors to the park will find picnic areas, hiking and bicycling trails, a boat ramp, fishing and swimming.

CACHE CREEK

Juniper Beach Provincial Park, located 20 kilometers east of Cache Creek on Highway 1, is a 260-hectare park offering picnic areas, hiking trails, fishing and swimming.

Marble Canyon Provincial Park is a 335-hectare park located 40 kilometers northwest of Cache Creek, off Highway 12. You will enjoy picnic areas, boating, fishing and swimming.

CAMPBELL RIVER

Elk Falls Provincial Park encompasses 1,087 hectares of parkland and is located 10 kilometers northwest of Campbell River, off Highway 28. The park offers picnic areas, hiking trails, fishing and swimming.

Strathcona Provincial Park encompasses 219,304 hectares of parkland, located 48.25 kilometers west of Campbell River via Highway 28. You will enjoy picnic areas, hiking trails, a boat ramp, fishing, swimming and both cross-country and downhill skiing.

CANAL FLATS

Whiteswan Lake Provincial Park consists of 1,994 hectares of parkland, located 25 kilometers south of Canal Flats, off Highway 93/95. Here are picnic areas, hiking trails, a boat ramp, fishing, swimming and winter sports.

CASSIAR

Boya Lake Provincial Park, located 40 kilometers northeast of Cassiar, off Highway 37, consists of 4,597 acres of parkland and offers picnic areas, a boat ramp, fishing and swimming.

CASTLEGAR

Champion Lakes Provincial Park encompasses 1,424 hectares of parkland, located 10 kilometers south of Castlegar, off Highway 3B. You will find picnic areas, hiking trails, a boat ramp, fishing, swimming, cross-country skiing and other winter sports.

CHASE

Adams Lake Provincial Park consists of 56 hectares of parkland, located 15 kilometers north of Chase, off Highway 1. The park offers boating, fishing and swimming.

CHETWYND

East Pine Provincial Park is a 14-hectare park located 30 kilometers east of Chetwynd on Highway 97. Visitors to the park will find picnic areas, a boat ramp, fishing and swimming.

Moberly Lake Provincial Park consists of 98 hectares and is 24 kilometers northwest of Chetwynd on Highway 29. The park offers picnic areas, hiking trails, a boat ramp, fishing and swimming.

CHILLIWACK

Chilliwack Lake Provincial Park, located 84 kilometers southeast of Chilliwack via an access road off Highway 1, is a 162-hectare park offering picnic areas, a boat ramp, fishing and swimming.

Cultus Lake Provincial Park consists of 656 hectares of parkland, located 11 kilometers southwest of Chilliwack, off Highway 1. You will find picnic areas, hiking trails, a boat ramp, fishing and swimming.

CHRISTINA LAKE

Texas Creek Provincial Park is a 112-hectare park located 5 kilometers east of Christina Lake on Highway 3. Enjoy picnic areas, hiking trails, fishing and swimming.

CLEARWATER

North Thompson River Provincial Park, located 5 kilometers south of Clearwater off Highway 5, is a 126-hectare park offering picnic areas, hiking trails, a boat ramp, fishing, winter sports and a visitor's center.

Spahats Creek Provincial Park is a 270-hectare park located 15 kilometers north of Highway 5 at Clearwater. The park offers picnic areas and hiking trails.

Wells Gray Provincial Park encompasses 529,748 hectares of parkland, located 30 kilometers north of Clearwater via an access road off Highway 5. Visitors to the park will find picnic areas, hiking and bicycling trails, horse rentals, a boat ramp, boat rentals, fishing, swimming, winter sports and a visitor's center.

CLINTON

Big Bear Lake Provincial Park encompasses 332 hectares of parkland, located 40 kilometers north of Clinton, off Highway 97. You will find picnic areas, hiking trails, a boat ramp, fishing and swimming.

Downing Provincial Park, located 16 kilometers southeast of Clinton off Highway 97, is a 100-hectare park offering picnicking, fishing and swimming.

CORTES ISLAND

Smelt Bay Provincial Park consists of 16 hectares on Cortes Island via ferry from Campbell River. Enjoy picnic areas, fishing and swimming.

COURTENAY

Miracle Beach Provincial Park is a 135-hectare park located 22.5 kilometers north of Courtenay, off Highway 19. You will enjoy hiking trails, fishing, swimming and a visitor's center.

CRANBROOK

Kikomun Creek Provincial Park encompasses 682 hectares of parkland, located 64 kilometers east of Cranbrook, via Highway 3, then 11 kilometers south to the park entrance. The park offers picnic areas, hiking and bicycling trails, a boat ramp, fishing and swimming.

Moyie Lake Provincial Park is a 90-hectare park located 19 kilometers south of Cranbrook on Highway 3. The park offers picnic areas, hiking trails, a boat ramp, fishing and swimming.

CRESTON

Lockhart Beach Provincial Park is a 3-hectare park, located 53 kilometers north of Creston on Highway 3A. Stop here for picnicking, fishing and swimming.

DENMAN ISLAND

Fillongley Provincial Park is a 23-hectare park located on Denman Island. The park is accessible via ferry from Buckley Bay and offers areas for picnicking, fishing and swimming.

FORT NELSON

Andy Bailey Provincial Park consists of 174 hectares, located 11 kilometers southeast of Highway 97, near Fort Nelson. The park offers picnic areas, a boat ramp, fishing and swimming.

Stone Mountain Provincial Park encompasses 25,691 hectares of parkland, located 125 kilometers north of Fort Nelson, on Highway 97. Visitors to the park will find picnic areas, hiking trails, boating, fishing and winter sports.

FORT SAINT JAMES

Paarens Beach Provincial Park, located 10 kilometers southwest of Fort Saint James off Highway 27, is a 43-hectare park offering picnic areas, hiking trails, a boat ramp, fishing and swimming.

Sowchea Bay Provincial Park consists of 13 hectares of parkland, located on Stuart Lake, 13 kilometers west of Fort Saint James, off Highway 27. The park offers a boat ramp, fishing and swimming.

FORT SAINT JOHN

Beatton Provincial Park is a 312-hectare park located 13 kilometers north of Highway 97 near Fort Saint John. You will find picnic areas, hiking and bicycling trails, a boat ramp, fishing, swimming, cross-country skiing and other winter sports.

Charlie Lake Provincial Park, located 13 kilometers northwest of Fort Saint John, off highway 97, is a 92-hectare park offering picnic areas, hiking trails, a boat ramp, fishing and swimming.

FORT STEELE

Norbury Lake Provincial Park is a 97-hectare park located southeast of the junction to Highways 93 and 95 at Fort Steele. Enjoy picnic areas, hiking trails, a boat ramp, fishing and swimming.

Wasa Lake Provincial Park encompasses 144 hectares of parkland located 21 kilometers north of Fort Steele, off Highway 93/95. Here you will find picnic areas, hiking trails, a boat ramp, fishing, swimming, winter sports and a nature program.

GALENA

Trout Lake Provincial Park, located 50 kilometers south of Galena on Highway 31, is a 316-hectare park offering picnic areas, hiking trails and fishing.

GALIANO ISLAND

Montague Harbour Marine Provincial Park, located 48 kilometers north of Victoria on Galiano Island via car ferry, is a 97-hectare park offering picnic areas, hiking trails, a boat ramp, fishing and swimming.

GIBSONS LANDING

Toberts Creek Provincial Park is a 40-hectare park located 10 kilometers west of Gibsons Landing on Highway 101. Visitors to the park will find picnic areas, a boat ramp, fishing and swimming.

GRAHAM ISLAND

Naikoon Provincial Park encompasses 72,641 hectares of parkland on the northern tip of Graham Island in the Queen Charlotte Islands. Enjoy picnic areas, hiking trails, a boat ramp, fishing and swimming.

HARRISON HOT SPRINGS

Sadquatch Provincial Park, located 6.4 kilometers north of Harrison Hot Springs via an access road off Highway 7, encompasses 1,217 hectares of parkland. You will find picnic areas, hiking trails, a boat ramp, fishing and swimming.

HARRISON MILLS

Kilby Provincial Park is a 3-hectare park located 2 kilometers east of Harrison Mills, on Highway 7. This historic park offers picnic areas, hiking trails, a boat ramp, fishing, swimming and a visitor's center.

HAZELTON

Seeley Lake Provincial Park, located 6 kilometers west of Hazelton on Highway 16, is a 24-hectare park offering picnic areas, boating, fishing and swimming.

HOPE

Manning Provincial Park encompasses 66,884 hectares of parkland, located on Highway 3, between Hope and Princeton. You will find picnic areas, hiking and bicycling trails, a boat ramp, boat rentals, fishing, swimming, winter sports and a visitor's center.

Skagit Valley Provincial Park consists of 32,508 hectares of parkland, located 8 kilometers west of Hope, via Highway 1, then 43 kilometers south on Second Road. The park offers boating, fishing, swimming and a visitor's center.

JORDAN RIVER

French Beach Provincial Park is a 59-hectare park located 5 kilometers east of Jordan River, off Highway 14. The park offers picnic areas, hiking trails, fishing and swimming.

KASLO

Kootenay Lake Provincial Park encompasses 343 hectares of parkland, located near Kaslo on Highway 31. Visitors to the park will find areas for picnicking, fishing and swimming.

KAMLOOPS

Lac Le Jeune Provincial Park, located 28 kilometers southwest of Kamloops off Highway 5, is a 47-hectare park offering picnic areas, hiking trails, a boat ramp, fishing, swimming and winter sports.

Paul Lake Provincial Park is a 402-hectare park located 25 kilometers northeast of Kamloops, off Highway 5. Enjoy the hiking trails, a boat ramp, fishing, swimming and winter sports.

KELOWNA

Bear Creek Provincial Park encompasses 178 hectares of parkland, located 8 kilometers north of Highway 97, near Kelowna. Visitors to the park will find picnic areas, hiking and bicycling trails, fishing and swimming.

KEREMEOS

Cathedral Provincial Park consists of 33,272 hectares of parkland, located 24 kilometers southwest of Keremeos, off Highway 3. The park offers hiking trails and fishing.

KIMBERLEY

Top of the World Provincial Park, located 95 kilometers east of Kimberley off Highway 93, then 54 kilometers east on the gravel access road, offers hiking trails, fishing, swimming and winter sports.

KINASKAN LAKE

Kinaskan Lake Provincial Park encompasses 1,800 hectares of parkland, located on Highway 37, at Kinaskan Lake. Enjoy the hiking trails, a boat ramp and fishing.

LAC LA HACHE

Lac la Hache Provincial Park is a 24-hectare park located 13 kilometers north of Lac la Hache on Highway 97. Here you will find a boat ramp, fishing, swimming and cross-country skiing.

LAKE COWICHAN

Gordon Bay Provincial Park, located 14 kilometers west of Lake Cowichan off Highway 18, is a 51-hectare park offering picnic areas, hiking trails, a boat ramp, fishing and swimming.

LIARD RIVER

Liard River Hotsprings Provincial Park encompasses 976 hectares of parkland at Liard River, located on Highway 97. The park offers picnic areas, hiking trails, swimming and winter sports.

MACKENZIE

Tudyah Lake Provincial Park is a 56-hectare park located on Highway 97 at Mackenzie. Visitors to the park will find picnic areas, a boat ramp, fishing and swimming.

MCLEOD LAKE

Carp Lake Provincial Park, located 32 kilometers southwest of McLeod Lake off Highway 97, encompasses 19,344 hectares of parkland and offers hiking and bicycling trails, a boat ramp, canoeing, fishing and swimming.

MAPLE RIDGE

Golden Ears Provincial Park consists of 55,594 hectares of parkland, located 11 kilometers northwest of Maple Ridge, off Highway 7. It offers hiking and bicycling trails, horse rentals, a boat ramp, fishing, swimming and winter sports.

MERRITT

Kentucky-Alleyne Provincial Park, located 30 kilometers south of Merritt on Highway 5A, is a 144-hectare park offering picnic areas, hiking trails, boating, fishing and swimming.

Monck Provincial Park, located 22 kilometers northeast of Merritt off Highway 5A, is an 87-hectare park offering picnic areas, hiking trails, a boat ramp, fishing and swimming.

MISSION

Rolley Lake Provincial Park encompasses 115 hectares of parkland, located 13 kilometers northwest of Mission, off Highway 7. Enjoy picnic areas, hiking trails, boating, fishing and swimming.

MUNCHO LAKE

Muncho Lake Provincial Park consists of 88,416 hectares of parkland on Highway 97, at Muncho Lake. The park offers picnic areas, hiking trails, a boat ramp, fishing, winter sports and a visitor's center.

NAKUSP

McDonald Creek Provincial Park encompasses 468 hectares of parkland, located 10 kilometers south of Nakusp, on Highway 23. Visitors to the park will find picnic areas, a boat ramp, fishing and swimming.

NELSON

Kokanee Creek Provincial Park is a 260-hectare park located 19 kilometers northeast of Nelson on Highway 3A. It offers hiking trails, a boat ramp, fishing, swimming, winter sports such as cross-country skiing and a visitor's center.

OSOYOOS

Conkle Lake Provincial Park encompasses 587 hectares of parkland located 28 kilometers northeast of Osoyoos, via Highway 3, then 26 kilometers to the park entrance. Here you will find hiking trails, a boat ramp, fishing and swimming.

Haynes Point Provincial Park, located 2 kilometers south of Osoyoos on Highway 97, is a 38-hectare park offering picnic areas, a boat ramp, fishing and swimming.

PARKSVILLE

Englishman River Falls Provincial Park, located 13 kilometers southwest of Parksville, off Highway 4, is a 97-hectare park offering picnic areas, hiking trails, fishing and swimming.

Little Qualicum Falls Provincial Park encompasses 444 hectares of parkland, located 13 kilometers southwest of Parksville, off Highway 4. Here you will find picnic areas, hiking trails, fishing and swimming.

Rathtrevor Beach Provincial Park is a 347-hectare park located 3 kilometers south of Parksville on Highway 19. Enjoy hiking trails, fishing, swimming and a visitor's center.

PEMBERTON

Birkenhead Lake Provincial Park consists of 3,642 acres of parkland located 55 kilometers northeast of Pemberton, off Highway 99. It offers picnic areas, hiking and bicycling trails, a boat ramp, fishing and swimming.

PENTICTON

Okanagan Lake Provincial Park, located 28 kilometers northwest of Penticton off Highway 97, is a 99-hectare park offering picnic areas, hiking trails, a boat ramp, fishing and swimming.

PORT ALBERNI

Sproat Lake Provincial Park is a 39-hectare park located 13 kilometers northwest of Port Alberni on Sproat Lake Road. Visitors to the park will find picnic areas, hiking trails, a boat ramp, fishing and swimming.

Stamp Falls Provincial Park, located 14 kilometers west of Port Alberni on Stamp River Road, is a 236-hectare park offering picnic areas, hiking trails and fishing.

Taylor Arm Provincial Park consists of 79 hectares of parkland located 15 kilometers west of Port Alberni, on Highway 4. Enjoy hiking and bicycling trails, boating and fishing.

PRINCE GEORGE

Beaumont Provincial Park encompasses 191 hectares of parkland on Fraser Lake, 129 kilometers west of Prince George off Highway 16. The park offers a boat ramp, fishing and swimming.

Crooked River Provincial Park is a 873-hectare park located 72 kilometers north of Prince George, on Highway 97, offering hiking and bicycling trails, year-round fishing, swimming and cross-country skiing.

Purden Lake Provincial Park encompasses 321 hectares of parkland, located 64 kilometers east of Prince George, off Highway 16. Visitors to the park will find picnic areas, hiking trails, a boat ramp, fishing, swimming and winter sports such as cross-country skiing and ice-fishing.

West Lake Provincial Park is a 258-hectare park located 29 kilometers southwest of Prince George, off Highway 16. The park offers a boat ramp, fishing, swimming and winter sports.

PRINCETON

Allison Lake Provincial Park, located 28 kilometers north of Princeton on Highway 5, is a 23-hectare park offering picnic areas, a boat ramp, fishing and swimming.

Bromley Rock Provincial Park encompasses 149 hectares of parkland located 19 kilometers east of Princeton, off Highway 3. The park offers areas for picnicking, fishing and swimming.

Otter Lake Provincial Park is a 51-hectare park located at Otter Lake, 25 kilometers west of Princeton, off Highway 5A. Here you will find picnic areas, a boat ramp, fishing and swimming.

QUADRA ISLAND

Rebecca Spit Provincial Park is a 177-hectare park on Quadra Island via ferry from Campbell River, then 5 kilometers east on Heriot Bay Road. The park offers picnic areas, a boat ramp, fishing and swimming.

QUESNEL

Ten-Mile Lake Provincial Park, located 10 kilometers north of Quesnel on Highway 97, consists of 253 hectares of parkland with picnic areas, hiking trails, a boat ramp, fishing, swimming and cross-country skiing.

RED PASS

Mount Robson Provincial Park, located near Red Pass, bordering Jasper National Park on Highway 16, is a 219,534-hectare park offering picnic areas, hiking and bicycling trails, horse rentals, a boat ramp, fishing, swimming, winter sports and a visitor's center.

REVELSTOKE

Blanket Creek Provincial Park is a 316-hectare park located 30 kilometers south of Revelstoke on Highway 23. A good choice for hiking and bicycling trails, it also has a boat ramp, boat rentals, fishing, swimming, winter sports and a visitor's center.

Downie Creek Provincial Park, located 70 kilometers north of Revelstoke on Highway 23, is a 100-hectare park offering picnic areas, a boat ramp, fishing and swimming.

Yard Creek Provincial Park encompasses 61 hectares of parkland, located 20 kilometers north of Revelstoke, on Highway 23. Visitors will find picnic areas, hiking trails, fishing and winter sports.

ROBSON

Syringa Creek Provincial Park, located 17 kilometers north of Robson off Highway 3, consists of 226 hectares of parkland offering picnic areas, hiking trails, a boat ramp, fishing and swimming.

ROCK CREEK

Kettle River Provincial Park consists of 179 hectares of parkland, located 5 kilometers north of Rock Creek, on Highway 33. Enjoy hiking trails, boating, fishing, swimming and winter sports.

ROSSLAND

Nancy Greene Provincial Park is a 203-hectare park, located 26 kilometers northwest of Rossland via Highway 3B. Visitors to the park will find picnic areas, hiking and bicycling trails, boating, fishing, swimming and winter sports, such as cross-country skiing and snowshoeing.

SALTSPRING ISLAND

Ruckle Provincial Park encompasses 486 hectares of parkland at Beaver Point on Saltspring Island, via ferry from Swartz Bay. The park offers picnic areas, hiking trails, fishing and swimming.

SALTERY BAY

Saltery Bay Provincial Park is a 69-hectare park located at Saltery Bay, west of the ferry landing at Highway 101. Enjoy hiking trails, a boat ramp, fishing and swimming.

SAYWARD

Schoen Lake Provincial Park encompasses 8,170 hectares of parkland, located 20 kilometers north of Sayward, then 12 kilometers south on Highway 19. The park offers hiking trails, boating and swimming.

SECHELT

Porpoise Bay Provincial Park, located 4 kilometers northeast of Sechelt on East Porpoise Bay Road, is a 62-hectare park offering picnic areas, hiking trails, boating, fishing and swimming.

SEYMOUR ARM

Silver Beach Provincial Park, located at the north end of Shuswap Lake at Seymour Arm, is a 130-hectare park offering picnic areas, hiking trails, boating, fishing and swimming.

SHELTER BAY

Arrow Lakes Provincial Park consists of 93 hectares of parkland, located on Highway 23 at Shelter Bay. It offers picnic areas, a boat ramp, fishing and swimming.

SKOOKUMCHUCK

Premier Lake Provincial Park, located 16 kilometers east of Skookumchuck via Highway 95, is a 662-hectare park offering picnic areas, a boat ramp, fishing, swimming and winter sports.

SPENCERS BRIDGE

Goldpan Provincial Park is a 5-hectare park located 10 kilometers south of Spencers Bridge on Highway 1. Visitors to the park will find areas for picnicking and fishing and for winter sports.

SQUAMISH

Alice Lake Provincial Park, located 13 kilometers north of Squamish on Highway 99, consists of 396 hectares. It has picnic areas, hiking and bicycling trails, boating, fishing, swimming, cross-country skiing, nature programs and a visitor's center.

SQUILAX

Roderick Haig-Brown Provincial Park encompasses 988 hectares of parkland, located 5 kilometers north of Highway 1 at Squilax. Enjoy picnic areas, hiking and bicycling trails, boating, fishing, swimming, winter sports and a visitor's center.

Shuswap Lake Provincial Park, located 19.25 kilometers north of Squilax, is a 149-hectare park that offers picnic areas, hiking trails, a boat ramp, fishing, swimming, a nature program, winter sports and a visitor's center.

STEWART

Meziadin Lake Provincial Park encompasses 335 hectares and is located 50 kilometers east of Stewart, off Highway 37. The park offers a boat ramp, fishing and swimming.

TAPPEN

Herald Provincial Park consists of 79 hectares of parkland, located 12.8 miles northeast of Tappen, off Highway 1. Visitors will find picnic areas, hiking trails, a boat ramp, fishing and swimming.

TELKWA

Tyhee Lake Provincial Park, located 8 kilometers west of Telkwa on Highway 16, is a 33-hectare park offering picnic areas, hiking trails, a boat ramp, fishing, swimming and winter sports such as cross-country skiing.

TERRACE

Exchamsiks River Provincial Park consists of 18 hectares of parkland located 57.9 kilometers west of Terrace, off Highway 16. You will find areas for picnicking, boating and fishing.

Lakelse Lake Provincial Park, located 26 kilometers southwest of Terrace on Highway 37, encompasses 362 hectares of parkland offering picnic areas, hiking trails, a boat ramp, fishing and swimming.

Kleanza Creek Provincial Park encompasses 269 hectares of parkland, located 20 kilometers from Terrace on Highway 16. Enjoy the hiking trails and fishing.

TOPLEY

Red Bluff Provincial Park, located 48 kilometers north of Topley via an access road, is a 148-hectare park offering picnic areas, hiking trails, a boat ramp, fishing and swimming.

Topley Provincial Park is a 12-hectare park located 40 kilometers north of Topley off Highway 16. The park offers picnic areas, fishing and swimming.

TRAIL

Beaver Creek Provincial Park is a 44-hectare park located 12.9 kilometers east of Trail on Highway 22A. Enjoy picnic areas, a boat ramp and fishing.

TUMBLER RIDGE

Gwillim Lake Provincial Park encompasses 9,199 hectares of parkland located 40 kilometers northwest of Tumbler Ridge on Highway 29. Visitors will find picnic areas, a boat ramp and fishing.

TUPPER

Swan Lake Provincial Park is a 67-hectare park located 38 kilometers south of Tupper via Highway 2. Enjoy hiking trails, a boat ramp, fishing, swimming and winter sports.

VANCOUVER

Mount Seymour Provincial Park is a 3,508-hectare park located 24 kilometers northeast of Vancouver off Highway 1. You will find picnic areas, hiking and bicycling trails and winter sports.

Porteau Cove Provincial Park consists of 50 hectares of parkland located 30 kilometers north of Vancouver on Highway 99. Enjoy picnic areas, a boat ramp, fishing, scuba diving and swimming.

VASSEUX

Vasseux Lake Provincial Park, located at Vasseux Lake on Highway 97, is a 12-hectare lake offering picnic areas, hiking trails, boating, fishing and swimming.

VERNON

Ellison Provincial Park, located 16 kilometers southwest of Vernon off Highway 97, is a 219-hectare park offering picnic areas, hiking trails, boating, fishing, swimming and winter sports.

Mabel Lake Provincial Park encompasses 182 hectares of parkland, located 76 kilometers northeast of Vernon via an access road off Highway 6. The park offers picnic areas, a boat ramp, fishing, swimming and winter sports.

Silver Star Provincial Park is a 6,092-hectare park located 22 kilometers east of Vernon on Silver Star Road. It offers hiking trails, a visitor's center and winter sports such as snowmobiling and cross-country and downhill skiing.

VICTORIA

Bamberton Provincial Park consists of 28 hectares of parkland, located 32 kilometers north of Victoria, off Highway 1. You will find areas for picnicking, fishing and swimming.

Goldstream Provincial Park, located 19.3 kilometers northwest of Victoria via Highway 1, is a 329-hectare park offering picnic areas, hiking trails, fishing, swimming, a visitor's center, and in the fall, the salmon spawn here.

WELLS

Barkerville Provincial Park encompasses 55 hectares of parkland located 8 kilometers east of Wells on Highway 26. Enjoy the hiking trails and visitor's center.

WHISTLER

Brandywine Falls Provincial Park, located 25 kilometers south of Whistler on Highway 99, is a 148-hectare park offering picnic areas, hiking trails, fishing and winter sports.

WILLIAMS LAKE

Tweedsmuir Provincial Park encompasses 994,246 hectares of parkland, located 349 kilometers northwest of Williams Lake. The park offers hiking trails, horse rentals, a boat ramp, boat rentals, fishing, swimming and winter sports.

Index

A Spokane Bed and Breakfast Service – Spokane, WA...135
Adams Lake Provincial Park – BC...202
Ainsworth State Park – OR...80
Alaska Hotel – Dawson Creek...167
Alderbrook Resort – Union, WA...141
Alexis Hotel – Seattle, WA...131
Alice Lake Provincial Park – BC...212
Allison Lake Provincial Park – BC...210
Alta Crystal Resort – Greenwater, WA...107
Alta Lake State Park – WA...155
Andy Bailey Provincial Park – BC...204
Applegate Lake – OR...74
Armitage State Park – OR...77
Arrow Lakes Provincial Park – BC...212
Ashwood Bed and Breakfast – Corvallis, OR...31
Austrian Chalet – Best Western – Campbell River, BC...163

Bamberton Provincial Park – BC...214
Barkerville Provincial Park – BC...214
Battle Ground Lake State Park – WA...149
Bay View State Park – WA...150
Beachside State Park – OR...82
Beacon Rock State Park – WA...157
Bear Creek Provincial Park – BC...206
Beatton Provincial Park – BC...205
Beaumont Provincial Park – BC...209
Beaver Creek Provincial Park – BC...213
Ben and Kay Dorris State Park – OR...77
Benson Hotel – Portland, OR...52
Benson State Park – OR...81
Best Western Inn – Ontario, OR...50
Beverly Beach State Park – OR...79
Big Bear Lake Provincial Park – BC...203
Big K Guest Ranch – Elkton, OR...32
Birch Bay State Park – WA...149
Birkenhead Lake Provincial Park – BC...209
Blake Island Marine State Park – WA...156
Blanket Creek Provincial Park – BC...210
Blue River Lake – OR...73
Blue Willow Bed and Breakfast Inn – Qualicum Beach, BC...178
Bogachiel State Park – WA...150

Bonnieville Lock and Dam – OR...74
Boya Lake Provincial Park – BC...202
Brandywine Falls Provincial Park – BC...214
Bridge Lake Provincial Park – BC...201
Bridgeport State Park – WA...150
British Columbia National Parks General Information...200
British Columbia Provincial Parks General Information...201
Bromley Rock Provincial Park – BC...210
Bullards Beach State Park – OR...75

Camano Island State Park – WA...150
Canim Beach Provincial Park – BC...201
Cape Arago State Park – OR...76
Cape Blanco State Park – OR...80
Cape Kiwanda State Park – OR...80
Cape Lookout State Park – OR...82
Carl G. Washburne Memorial State Park – OR...77
Carp lake Provincial Park – BC...207
Cascade Inn – Best Western – Winthrop, WA...147
Cascadia State Park – OR...82
Casey State Park – OR...79
Cathedral Provincial Park – BC...207
Catherine Creek State Park – OR...82
Cavanaugh's River Inn – Spokane, WA...136
Cedar House Inn Bed and Breakfast – Point Roberts, WA...119
Central Ferry State Park – WA...155
Champion Lakes Provincial Park – BC...202
Champoeg State Park – OR...79
Charlie Lake Provincial Park – BC...205
Chief Timothy State Park – WA...151
Chilliwack Lake Provincial Park – BC...203
Cinnamon Rabbit Bed and Breakfast – Olympia, WA...117
Clyde Holliday State Park – OR...78
Coast Hospitality Inn – Port Alberni, BC...177
College Way Inn – Best Western – Mount Vernon, WA...112
Collier Memorial State Park – OR...76
Columbia Gorge Hotel – Hood River, OR...42

Comfort Inn – Boardwalk – Seaside, OR...59
Comfort Inn – Walla Walla, WA...145
Conconully State Park – WA...155
Conkle Lake Provincial Park – BC...208
Coos Bay Manor – Coos Bay, OR...30
Cottage Grove Reservoir – OR...73
Cotton Tree Inn – Best Western – Mount Vernon, WA...113
Cougar Lake – OR...73
Coulee Dam National Recreation Area – WA...148
Country Inn – La Conner, WA...110
Country Place – McKenzie Bridge, OR...47
Courtesy Inn – Kamloops, BC...169
Cove Palisades State Park – OR...78
Crater Lake National Park – OR...70
Crooked River Provincial Park – BC...209
Crowne Plaza Hotel – Lake Oswego, OR...44
Cultus Lake Provincial Park – BC...203
Curlew Lake State Park – WA...156

Dabney State Park – OR...81
Daroga State Park – WA...155
Dash Point State Park – WA...157
Dashwood Seaside Manor Bed and Breakfast Inn – Victoria, BC...193
Deception Pass State Park – WA...154
Delta Vancouver Airport Hotel and Marina – Richmond, BC...182
Delta Whistler Resort – Whistler, BC...198
Der Ritterhof Motor Inn – Leavenworth, WA...111
Deschutes National Forest – OR...71
Deschutes River State Park – OR...82
Detroit Lake – OR...73
Detroit Lake State Park – OR...76
Devil's Elbow State Park – OR...77
Devil's Lake State Park – OR...78
Dexter Lake – OR...73
Dorena Reservoir – OR...73
Dosewallips State Park – WA...150
DoubleTree Hotel – Eugene-Springfield, OR...61
DoubleTree Hotel – Pendleton, OR...51
DoubleTree Hotel – Port Angeles, WA...120
Dougs Beach State Park – WA...153
Downie Creek Provincial Park – BC...210
Downing Provincial Park – BC...203

East Pine Provincial Park – BC...203
Ecola Creek Lodge – Cannon Beach, OR...27
Ecola State Park – OR...76

Edgewater Cottages – Waldport, OR...65
Edgewater Lodge – Whistler, BC...199
Edmonds Harbor Inn – Edmonds, WA...99
Elijah Bristow State Park – OR...77
Elk Falls Provincial Park – BC...202
Ellison Provincial Park – BC...214
Emigrant Springs State Park – OR...79
Englishman River Falls Provincial Park – BC...208
Ethel F. Wilson Memorial Provincial Park – BC...201
Exchamsiks River Provincial Park – BC...213

Fall Creek Lake – OR...74
Farewell Bend State Park – OR...78
Fay Bainbridge State Park – WA...158
Federal Way Executel – Best Western – Federal Way, WA...100
Fern Ridge Reservoir – OR...74
Fields Spring State Park – WA...149
Fifth Avenue Suites Hotel – Portland, OR...53
Filalgo Country Inn – Anacortes, WA...87
Fillongley Provincial Park – BC...204
Flaming Geyser State Park – WA...149
Flying M Ranch – Yamhill, OR...69
Fogarty Creek – OR...76
Fort Canby State Park – WA...153
Fort Casey State Park – WA...151
Fort Ebey State Park – WA...154
Fort Flagler State Park – WA...156
Fort Reading Bed and Breakfast – Hereford, OR...40
Fort Simcoe State Park – WA...158
Fort Stevens State Park – OR...78
Fort Ward State Park – WA...158
Fort Worden State Park – WA...156
Foster Lake – OR...74
Four Seasons Olympic Hotel – Seattle, WA...132
Fremont National Forest – OR...72
French Beach Provincial Park – BC...206
French Beach Retreats and Ocean Tree House – Sooke, BC...184

Georgian Court Hotel – Vancouver, BC...187
Gifford Pinchot National Forest – WA...148
Glacier National Park – BC...200
Golden and Silver Falls State Park – OR...76
Golden Ears Provincial Park – BC...207
Goldendale State Park – WA...152
Goldpan Provincial Park – BC...212
Goldstream Provincial Park – BC...214
Goose Lake State Park – OR...78

Gordon Bay Provincial Park – BC...207

Govenor Patterson Memorial State Park – OR...83

Grayland Beach State Park – WA...152

Green Lake Provincial Park – BC...201

Green Peter Lake – OR...75

Greenwood Inn – Beaverton, OR...23

Gwillim Lake Provincial Park – BC...213

Hallmark Inn – Best Western – Hillsboro, OR...41

Hallmark Resort – Cannon Beach, OR...28

Hanford House – DoubleTree Hotel – Richland, WA...129

Harbor Pointe Bed and Breakfast – Oak Harbor, WA...114

Harbour Towers Hotel – Victoria, BC...194

Harbourview Days Inn – Nanaimo, BC...175

Harris Beach State Park – OR...76

Harrison Hot Springs Hotel – Harrison Hot Springs, BC...168

Hat Rock State Park – OR...82

Haynes Point Provincial Park – BC...208

Hells Canyon National Recreation Area – OR...70

Hendricks Bridge State Park – OR...77

Herald Provincial Park – BC...212

Heritage Inn – Best Western – Pullman, WA...126

Heritage Inn – Best Western – Ritzville, WA...130

Heritage Inn – Best Western – Wenatchee, WA...146

Highland House – Clarkston, WA...92

Hilgard Junction State Park – OR...77

Hills Creek Lake – OR...74

Holiday Inn – Chilliwack, BC...165

Holiday Inn – Vancouver Centre – Vancouver, BC...188

Holiday Inn Express – Pullman, WA...127

Holiday Inn Express – Woodburn, OR...68

Holiday Inn Hotel and Suites – Vancouver Downtown – Vancouver, BC...189

Home by the Sea Cottages – Clinton, WA...94

Hood River Hotel – Hood River, OR...43

Horsefly Lake Provincial Park – BC...201

Horsethief Lake State Park – WA...158

Hotel Vintage Plaza – Portland, OR...54

Howard Johnson Inn – Kent, WA...108

Humbug Mountain State Park – OR...80

Idabel Lake Resort – Kelowna, BC...173

Ike Kinswa State Park – WA...154

Illahee State Park – WA...150

Inn at Friday Harbor – Friday Harbor, WA...103

Inn at Ludlow Bay – Port Ludlow, WA...123

Inn of the Sea Resort – Ladysmith, BC...174

Island Country Inn – Bainbridge Island, WA...89

Jackson F. Kimball State Park – OR...78

Jarrell Cove State Park – WA...156

Jessie M. Honeyman Memorial State Park – OR...77

Joemma Beach State Park – WA...153

John Day Lock and Dam – OR...74

Joseph P. Stewart State Park – OR...79

Jot's Resort – Gold Beach, OR...36

Juniper Beach Provincial Park – BC...202

Kalaloch Lodge – Forks, WA...102

Kanaskat–Palmer State Park – WA...152

Kentucky–Alleyne Provincial Park – BC...208

Kettle River Provincial Park – BC...211

Kikomun Creek Provincial Park – BC...204

Kilby Provincial Park – BC...206

Kinaskan Lake Provincial Park – BC...207

Kitsap Memorial State Park – WA...156

Kleanza Creek Provincial Park – BC...213

Kokanee Creek Provincial Park – BC...208

Kootenay Lake Provincial Park – BC...206

Kootenay National Parks – BC...200

Kopachuck State Park – WA...157

La Pine State Park – OR...78

La Quinta Inn – Kirkland, WA...109

Lac la Hache Provincial Park – BC...207

Lac Le Jeune Provincial Park – BC...206

Lac Le Jeune Resort – Kamloops, BC...170

Lake Chelan State Park – WA...151

Lake City Motor Inn – Burnaby, BC...162

Lake Cushman State Park – WA...152

Lake Easton State Park – WA...152

Lake Owyhee State Park – OR...80

Lake Quinault Lodge – Quinault, WA...128

Lake Sammamish State Park – WA...153

Lake Sylvia State Park – WA...153

Lake Wenatchee State Park – WA...153

Lakelse Lake Provincial Park – BC...213

Larrabee State Park – WA...149

Lewis and Clark State Park – OR...81

Lewis and Clark State Park – WA...150

Lewis and Clark Trail State Park – WA...151

Liard River Hotsprings Provincial Park – BC...207

Lincoln Rock State Park – WA...158

Little Qualicum Falls Provincial Park – BC...209
Llama Ranch Bed and Breakfast – Trout Lake, WA...140
Lockhart Beach Provincial Park – BC...204
Loeb State Park – OR...76
Log Cabin Resort – Port Angeles, WA...121
Lookout Point Lake – OR...73
Lost Creek Lake – OR...74
Love's Victorian Bed and Breakfast – Deer Park, WA...98
Lyon's Ferry State Park – WA...157

Mabel Lake Provincial Park – BC...214
Malheur National Forest – OR...72
Manchester State Park – WA...155
Manning Provincial Park – BC...206
Map – British Columbia...160
Map – Oregon...18
Map – Washington...84
Maple Rose Inn – Port Angeles, WA...122
Marble Canyon Provincial Park – BC...202
Maria Rose Bed and Breakfast – Vernon, BC...192
Marriott Downtown – Portland, OR...55
Mary S. Young State Park – OR...77
Maryhill State Park – WA...152
Mayer State Park – OR...82
McDonald Creek Provincial Park – BC...208
McNary Lock and Dam – OR...75
Meziadin Lake Provincial Park – BC...212
Millersylvania State Park – WA...155
Milo McIver State Park – OR...77
Minam State Park – OR...77
Miracle Beach Provincial Park – BC...204
Moberly Lake Provincial Park – BC...203
Monck Provincial Park – BC...208
Montague Harbour Marine Provincial Park – BC...205
Moran State Park – WA...154
Morrison Cottage – Mill City, OR...49
Moses Lake State Park – WA...154
Mount Hood Inn – Government Camp, OR...38
Mount Hood National Forest – OR...72
Mount Revelstoke National Park – BC...200
Mount Robson Provincial Park – BC...210
Mount Seymour Provincial Park – BC...213
Mount Spokane State Park – WA...157
Mount View Inn – Buckley, WA...91
Moyie Lake Provincial Park – BC...204
Mukilteo State Park – WA...154
Muncho Lake Provincial Park – BC...208

Naikoon Provincial Park – BC...205
Nancy Greene Provincial Park – BC...211
National Forest General Information – OR...71
National Parks General Information – OR...70
Nehalem Bay State Park – OR...79
Neptune State Park – OR...83
New Oregon Motel – Best Western – Eugene, OR...33
Nolte State Park – WA...152
Norbury Lake Provincial Park – BC...205
North Santiam State Park – OR...79
North Thompson River Provincial Park – BC...203

Ocean City State Park – WA...154
Ocean Locomotion On the Beach – Rockaway Beach, OR...57
Ocean Pointe Resort Hotel & Spa – Victoria, BC...195
Ocean View Resort – Best Western – Seaside, OR...60
Ocean Wilderness Inn and Spa Retreat – Sooke, BC...185
Ochoco Lake State Park – OR...81
Ochoco National Forest – OR...73
Okanagan Lake Provincial Park – BC...209
Olalla Orchard Bed and Breakfast – Olalla, WA...116
Old Brook Inn – Anacortes, WA...88
Old Dutch Inn – Qualicum Beach, BC...179
Old Fort Townsend State Park – WA...156
Old Welches Inn Bed and Breakfast – Welches, OR...67
Olympic National Forest – WA...148
Ona Beach State Park – OR...80
Ontario State Park – OR...80
Oregon Dunes National Recreation Area – OR...70
Oregon State Parks General Information...75
Osoyoos Lake State Park – WA...155
Oswald West State Park – OR...79
Otter Lake Provincial Park – BC...210
Oxford Castle Inn – Victoria, BC...196

Paarens Beach Provincial Park – BC...204
Pacific Beach State Park – WA...155
Pacific Rim National Park – BC...201
Palace Hotel – Port Townsend, WA...124
Paradise Point State Park – WA...157
Paul Lake Provincial Park – BC...206
Pearrygin Lake State Park – WA...158
Pendleton Bay Provincial Park – BC...202

Pendrell Suites – Vancouver, BC…190

Penrose Point State Park – WA…153

Phoenix Inn – Salem, OR…58

Pine Valley Lodge – Halfway, OR…39

Pony Soldier Inn – Albany, OR…21

Porpoise Bay Provincial Park – BC…211

Porteau Cove Provincial Park – BC…214

Potholes State Park – WA…154

Potlatch State Park – WA…157

Premier Lake Provincial Park – BC…212

Prineville Reservoir State Park – OR…81

Prospect Wayside State Park – OR…79

Puget View Guesthouse – Olympia, WA…118

Purden Lake Provincial Park – BC…209

Purple House Bed and Breakfast – Dayton, WA…96

Quaaout Lodge – Chase, BC…164

Quality Inn – Bremerton, WA…90

Quality Inn – The Dalles, OR…63

Rainbow Falls State Park – WA…150

Rathtrevor Beach Provincial Park – BC…209

Rebecca Spit Provincial Park – BC…210

Red Bluff Provincial Park – BC…213

Red Lion Inn – Bend North – Bend, OR…24

Renaissance Vancouver Hotel – Harbourside – Vancouver, BC…191

Residence Inn by Marriott – Fairview Avenue North – Seattle, WA…133

River Place Hotel – Portland, OR…56

Riverhouse Resort – Bend, OR…25

Riverside State Park – WA…157

Roderick Haig–Brown Provincial Park – BC…212

Rodeway Inn – Springfield, OR…62

Rogue River National Forest – OR…72

Rolley Lake Provincial Park – BC…208

Rooster Rock State Park – OR…81

Royal Coachman Inn – Tacoma/Fife, WA…138

Ruckle Provincial Park – BC…211

Sacajawea State Park – WA…155

Saddle Mountain State Park – OR…79

Sadquatch Provincial Park – BC…205

Salish Lodge and Spa – Snoqualmie, WA…134

Salishan Lodge – Gleneden Beach, OR…35

Saltery Bay Provincial Park – BC…211

Saltwater State Park – WA…151

Samuel H. Boardman State Park – OR…76

Sand 'n Sea Motel – Gold Beach, OR…37

Scenic Beach State Park – WA…150

Schafer State Park – WA…156

Schoen Lake Provincial Park – BC…211

Sea Dreamer Inn – Brookings, OR…26

Sea Horse Oceanfront Lodging – Lincoln City, OR…45

Seal Rock Wayside State Park – OR…80

Seaquest State Park – WA…150

Seeley Lake Provincial Park – BC…206

Sequim Bay State Park – WA…156

Shelton Wayside State Park – OR…82

Shilo Inn – Downtown – Vancouver, WA…142

Shilo Inn – Hazel Dell – Vancouver, WA…143

Shilo Inn – Medford, OR…48

Shilo Inn – Tacoma/Fife, WA…139

Shilo Inn – Warrenton, OR…66

Shuswap Lake Provincial Park – BC…212

Silver Beach Provincial Park – BC…211

Silver Falls State Park – OR…82

Silver Star Provincial Park – BC…214

Siskiyou National Forest – OR…72

Siulaw National Forest – OR…71

Skagit Valley Provincial Park – BC…206

Smelt Bay Provincial Park – BC…204

Smith Rock State Park – OR…81

Sonia's Bed and Breakfast by the Sea – Victoria, BC…197

Sooke Harbour House…186

South Beach State Park – OR…80

South Fork Moorage – Guest Houseboats – Fir Island, WA…101

South Whidbey State Park – WA…151

Sowchea Bay Provincial Park – BC…204

Spahats Creek Provincial Park – BC…203

Spencer Spit State Park– WA…153

Sproat Lake Provincial Park – BC…209

Squilchuck State Park – WA…158

Stamp Falls Provincial Park – BC…209

Steamboat Rock State Park – WA…152

Stewart Lodge – Cle Elum, WA…93

Stone Mountain Provincial Park – BC…204

Strathcona Provincial Park – BC…202

Succor Creek State Park – OR…80

Sucia Island State Park – WA..154.

Sumpter Valley Dredge State Park – OR…75

Sun Lakes State Park – WA…151

Sunset Bay State Park – OR…80

Sunset Vacation Rentals – Manzanita, OR…46

Sunset View Resort – Ocean Park, WA…115

Surfsand Resort – Cannon Beach, OR…29

Swallow's Nest Guest Cottages – Vashon Island, WA…144

Swan Hotel and Conference Center – Port Townsend, WA…125
Swan Lake Provincial Park – BC…213
Syringa Creek Provincial Park – BC…211

Taylor Arm Provincial Park – BC…209
Ten Mile Lake Provincial Park – BC…210
Texas Creek Provincial Park – BC…203
The Chalet – Radium Hot Springs, BC…180
The Dalles Lock and Dam – OR…75
Thompson Hotel – Kamloops, BC…171
Thunderbird Inn – Best Western – Spokane, WA…137
Tigh–Na–Mara Resort Hotel – Parksville, BC…176
Toberts Creek Provincial Park – BC…205
Tolmie State Park – WA…154
Top of the World Provincial Park – BC…207
Topley Provincial Park – BC…213
Tou Velle State Park – OR…79
Travelodge – Chilliwack, BC…166
Trout Lake Provincial Park – BC…205
Tryon Creek State Park – OR…81
Tucker House Bed and Breakfast with Cottages – Friday Harbor, WA…104
Tudyah Lake Provincial Park – BC…207
Tumalo State Park – OR…75
Twanoh State Park – WA…157
Tweedsmuir Provincial Park – BC…214
Twenty–five Mile Creek State Park – WA…151
Twin Harnors State Park – WA…158
Tyhee Lake Provincial Park – BC…213

Umatilla National Forest – OR…72
Umpqua Lighthouse State Park – OR…81
Umpqua National Forest – OR…73
Umpqua Wayside State Park – OR…81
Unity Lake State Park – OR…82

Valley of the Rogue State Park – OR…81

Valley River Inn – Eugene, OR…34
Vasseux Lake Provincial Park – BC…214
Victorian Bed and Breakfast – Coupeville, WA…95

Waddling Dog – Quality Inn – Saanichton, BC…183
Wallace Falls State Park – WA…152
Wallowa Lake State Park – OR…78
Wallowa-Whitman National Forest – OR…
Wanapum State Park – WA…157
Wasa Lake Provincial Park – BC…205
Washington National Forests and Parks General Information…148
Washington State Parks General Information…149
Wayfarer Resort – Vida, OR…64
Wayside Inn – Best Western – Revelstoke, BC…181
Weinhard Hotel – Dayton, WA…97
Wells Gray Provincial Park – BC…203
Wenatchee Confluence State Park – WA…158
Wenberg State Park – WA…153
West Lake Provincial Park – BC…210
West Winds Harmony Cottage – Friday Harbor, WA…105
Wharfside Bed and Breakfast Aboard the "Jacquelyn" – Friday Harbor, WA…106
Whiteswan Lake Provincial Park – BC…202
Willamette Mission State Park – OR…82
Willamette National Forest – OR…71
William H. Tugman State Park – OR…76
Windmill's Ashland Hills Inn and Suites – Ashland, OR…22
Winema National Forest – OR…72
Woody Life Village Resort – Kamloops, BC…172

Yakima Sportsmen's State Park – WA..159
Yard Creek Provincial Park – BC…211
Yoho National Park – BC…200

About the Author... from a dog's point of view

Dreamer Dawg, office manager and "cover girl" for Bon Vivant Press, is a ten-year-young Labrador Retriever. When not exploring the food and lodging for each regional book, you can find Dreamer relaxing onboard her boat in the Monterey harbor or running with the horses in the Salinas Valley.

Owners Kathleen & Robert Fish, authors of the popular "Secrets" series, have researched and written twenty-one award-winning cookbooks and travel books, and are always on the lookout for lodgings with style and character.

Other titles in the Pets Welcome™ series are *Pets Welcome™ California, Pets Welcome™ America's South, Pets Welcome™ New England, Pets Welcome™* Southwest and *Pets Welcome™ National Edition.*

Bon Vivant Press

A division of The Millennium Publishing Group
PO Box 1994, Monterey, CA 93942
800-524-6826 • 831-373-0592 • 831-373-3567 FAX • Website: www.millpub.com

Send _____ copies of "Pets Welcome™ America's South" at $15.95 each.
Send _____ copies of "Pets Welcome™ California" at $15.95 each.
Send _____ copies of "Pets Welcome™ New England" at $15.95 each.
Send _____ copies of "Pets Welcome™ Pacific Northwest" at $15.95 each.
Send _____ copies of "Pets Welcome™ Southwest" at $15.95 each.
Send _____ copies of "Pets Welcome™ National Edition" at $19.95 each.

Add $4.50 postage and handling for the first book ordered and $1.50 for each additional book. Please add 7.25% sales tax per book, for those books shipped to California addresses.

Please charge my ☐ Visa ☐ MasterCard   # _____

Expiration date _____ Signature _____

Enclosed is my check for _____

Name _____

Address _____

City _____ State _____ Zip _____

☐ **This is a gift. Send directly to:**

Name _____

Address _____

City _____ State _____ Zip _____

☐ **Autographed by the author**

Autographed to _____

Bon Vivant Press

A division of The Millennium Publishing Group
PO Box 1994, Monterey, CA 93942
800-524-6826 • 831-373-0592 • 831-373-3567 FAX • Website: www.millpub.com

Send _____ copies of "Cooking With the Masters of Food & Wine" at $34.95 each.
Send _____ copies of "The Elegant Martini" at $17.95 each.
Send _____ copies of "California Wine Country Cooking Secrets" at $14.95 each.
Send _____ copies of "Cape Cod's Cooking Secrets" at $14.95 each.
Send _____ copies of "Cooking Secrets for Healthy Living" at $15.95 each.
Send _____ copies of "Cooking Secrets From America's South" at $15.95 each.
Send _____ copies of "Cooking Secrets From Around the World" at $15.95 each.
Send _____ copies of "Florida's Cooking Secrets" at $15.95 each.
Send _____ copies of "The Gardener's Cookbook" at $15.95 each.
Send _____ copies of "The Great California Cookbook" at $14.95 each.
Send _____ copies of "The Great Vegetarian Cookbook" at $15.95 each.
Send _____ copies of "Jewish Cooking Secrets From Here and Far" at $14.95 each.
Send _____ copies of "Louisiana Cooking Secrets" at $15.95 each.
Send _____ copies of "Monterey's Cooking Secrets" at $13.95 each.
Send _____ copies of "New England's Cooking Secrets" at $14.95 each.
Send _____ copies of "Pacific Northwest Cooking Secrets" at $15.95 each.
Send _____ copies of "San Francisco's Cooking Secrets" at $13.95 each.
Send _____ copies of "Vegetarian Pleasures" at $19.95 each.

Add $4.50 postage and handling for the first book ordered and $1.50 for each additional book. Please add 7.25% sales tax per book, for those books shipped to California addresses.

Please charge my ☐ Visa ☐ MasterCard # _____

Expiration date _____ Signature _____
Enclosed is my check for _____
Name _____
Address _____
City _____ State _____ Zip _____

☐ **This is a gift. Send directly to:**
Name _____
Address _____
City _____ State _____ Zip _____

☐ **Autographed by the author**
Autographed to _____

Reader's Response Card

Please return to:
   Bon Vivant Press
   P.O. Box 1994
   Monterey, CA 93942
   Fax your information to: (831) 373-3567

Please assist us in updating our next edition. If you have discovered an interesting or charming inn, hotel, guest ranch, or spa in the Pacific Northwest area that allows pets, or any special neighborhood parks that allow pets, with or without a leash, please let us hear from you and include the following information:

Type of lodging: (circle one)   Bed and Breakfast, Hotel, Inn, Guest Ranch or Spa.

Lodging Name: _____

Lodging Address: _____

City:_____ State:_____ Zip Code: _____

Phone: _____

Comments: _____

_____

_____

Park Name: _____

Address or Cross Streets: _____

City:_____ State:_____ Zip Code: _____

Phone: (if known) _____ Leashes required? Yes / No

Comments: _____

_____

_____

We appreciate your assistance. It is wonderful to discover new and interesting places to take your pets. If you have discovered an interesting or charming inns, hotels, guest ranches, or spas in other states that allows pets, and any special neighborhood parks, please let us hear know for future editions.